THE UNITED STATES

BY MARCUS WEBB

LUCENT BOOKS
P.O. BOX 289011
SAN DIEGO, CA 92198-9011

TITLES IN THE MODERN NATIONS OF THE WORLD SERIES INCLUDE:

Brazil	Greece	Russia
Canada	India	Somalia
China	Ireland	South Africa
Cuba	Italy	South Korea
Egypt	Japan	Spain
England	Kenya	Sweden
Germany	Mexico	The United States

Library of Congress Cataloging-in-Publication Data

Webb, Marcus.
    The United States / by Marcus Webb.
        p.   cm. — (Modern nations of the world)
    Includes bibliographical references and index.
    Summary: Discusses the geography, history, people, and culture of the
United States and its significance in the world today.
    ISBN 1-56006-663-6 (lib. : alk. paper)
    1. United States—Juvenile literature. [1. United States.] I. Title.   II.
Series.
    E156.W43 2000

                                                                            99-39422
    CIP

Copyright © 2000 by Lucent Books, Inc.
P.O. Box 289011, San Diego, CA 92198-9011
Printed in the U.S.A.

CONTENTS

INTRODUCTION

THE UNITED STATES: A NATION OF NATIONS

The population of the United States includes 270 million people of all races, religions, and ethnic and national origins. These diverse peoples speak hundreds of languages. They perform thousands of different types of jobs, eat many different types of foods, and enjoy different types of music and art. They may worship different gods—or none. For these reasons, America and its people are sometimes called a nation of nations.

Nevertheless, the people of the United States live together in a unified country. They believe in the dignity of the individual, in human rights, in representative self-government, and in liberty through law. These ideals make the diverse population of the United States into a single citizenry: Americans. This fact is reflected in the national motto "E Pluribus Unum," which is Latin for "From Many, One." America itself is often described as a melting pot, blending all sorts of people into a single, yet diverse, national identity. In more recent years, U.S. society has also been referred to as a salad bowl since its mixture of different elements adds up to a distinctive whole, yet each element retains its unique individuality.

The U.S. national identity, sometimes called the American character, is easy to see in action. Americans are bold: They like to try new things. The American nation itself was founded as a deliberate experiment in self-rule. Americans are creative: They built the first working airplane, perfected motion pictures, developed the Internet, and invented a thousand other devices that drive their own and the world's economies and improve the lives of people everywhere.

Americans have their share of flaws, of course. Often, they have been accused of worshiping money and physicality while undervaluing intellectual or spiritual concerns and failing to use their great wealth to solve pressing social problems. American self-congratulation has been known to lead to complacency and stagnation. Also, U.S. citizens have sometimes focused so narrowly on domestic concerns that they ignore much of the outside world. Finally, Americans' bold optimism occasionally risks veering into arrogant naïveté.

At just over two hundred years old, America is a relatively young country. The faults of national adolescence are no doubt regrettable; but they may also be inseparable from the strengths of youth—enthusiasm, vitality, and hopefulness. Americans combine pride in their country with a marked willingness to be self-critical.

A cartoon satirizes the influx of immigrants to the United States in the 1800s. Immigrants flocked to the United States, attracted by the prospect of opportunity and personal liberty.

THE AMERICAN LAND: AS DIVERSE AS ITS PEOPLE

Geographically, the United States is also a nation of nations. The land Americans live on—three thousand miles from coast to coast and bolstered by the Hawaiian Islands and Alaskan wilderness—is as diverse as the people who live there. The United States includes almost every type of topography and climate found on the globe.

In the western part of the country, chains of mighty snow-capped mountains reach summits of fourteen thousand feet. The center of the nation includes broad plains that stretch for hundreds of miles. Some of these plains are dry and desertlike; other sections, including "the heartland," offer rich and fertile soil where farmers grow enough food to supply the nation and the world.

The rugged, snow-covered terrain of the Rocky Mountains in Colorado is one example of the diversity of landscapes and climates in the United States.

America includes subtropical jungle islands and beaches near the equator, yet it also contains frozen wastelands and glaciers near the North Pole. Altogether, the American landscape has proved rich in natural resources, including petroleum, gold, silver, uranium, coal, iron ore, zinc, timber, and abundant fish and wildlife. Linking this huge country with its

Beachgoers relax at Laguna Beach in southern California, a part of the country famed for its sun, sand, and surf.

dramatically different types of terrain are continually grow-ing arrays of human-made transportation and communica-tion systems.

The United States, then, is a rich and powerful nation whose diverse yet unified people see themselves as enjoying a great, ongoing adventure. America's adventure means a constant challenge and quest to create a better, stronger na-tion in a safer, more just world. U.S. citizens often speak of the American dream: the hope that all people may live to-gether happily and peacefully, and that each individual can have the opportunity to achieve his or her own best destiny.

The American Experiment: "A Republic— If You Can Keep It"

For most of human history—and indeed, in much of the world today—to be accepted as a citizen of a country meant that a person had to be born there. Or, perhaps to be a citizen one had to belong to a certain race, ethnic group, or religion. In some countries, on the other hand, citizenship merely means that an individual happens to live in that country and pay taxes.

The United States is different. People of all races, creeds, and ethnic backgrounds can become American citizens. They can enjoy the full rights and privileges of citizenship. As opposed to some other countries that may have religious or ethnic citizenship requirements or require new citizens to be married to native-born citizens, almost anyone can become an American.

Although the vast majority of Americans are citizens by birth, the nation's immigration laws and ceremonies provide evidence that being an American means agreeing with a certain set of ideas. When a citizen of another country becomes a U.S. citizen, he or she swears an oath of allegiance to the U.S. government and to certain ideals that that government represents. These include the idea that people can live together in freedom and the idea that people can be governed by themselves—not by a king, a dictator, or the head of an official religion. The American ideal includes the beliefs that all people deserve equal treatment under the law and can govern themselves under a set of laws that they create and administer through their elected representatives.

In addition, being an American means agreeing that not only are all people able to do these things, but all people are born with the right to freedom, justice, and self-government. And so, in America, the government is viewed as the people's servant, not their master. The individual, rather than any church, king, or government, is the source of power and the basic unit of society. The individual's rights come first; they cannot be taken away.

"Becoming an American citizen was truly a philosophical step for me," said Lorenzo Dalla Vedova, an Italian-born immigrant who was naturalized in June 1999.

You are potentially an American citizen from birth if you believe in certain principles that are central to the American way of life. Freedom is paramount. Becoming

A photo, taken about 1930, shows a family of recent arrivals gazing at the Statue of Liberty, a landmark countless other immigrants observed as they approached New York.

an American also means embracing the ideal of equality. It means being part of an always-evolving democracy. I believe that by becoming an American citizen, I can help preserve and improve this democracy.[1]

Like other new U.S. citizens, Dalla Vedova received a congratulatory letter from the U.S. president that stated, in part, "You now share in a great experiment: a nation dedicated to the ideal that all of us are created equal; a nation with profound respect for individual rights."[2]

When America was founded more than two hundred years ago, these were revolutionary ideas. America's first president, George Washington, was also the first to speak of the new nation as an experiment—a test to see whether people could govern themselves. In fact, these ideas and principles of American democracy were so revolutionary that the new nation struggled for many decades before it could include all of its people as equal citizens who participate fully in the benefits of freedom. In many respects, that struggle is still going on today. How did this revolutionary society come to be founded? It happened as the result of a mixture of many peoples and many ideas—sometimes cooperating, sometimes clashing—all of whom added their unique contributions to the culture and nation that eventually emerged as the United States of America.

THE FIRST AMERICANS

A visitor to North America in the 1400s would have found the continent already inhabited by an estimated 2 million people. These people, who were destined to play a large role in shaping the United States, lived in hundreds of independent tribal societies, including the Iroquois, Cherokee, Navajo, Lakota (Sioux), and Comanche. Some were nomadic hunter-gatherers; others lived in permanent communities and cultivated a wide variety of crops, including corn, beans, and squash.

Around the year 1000, Viking explorers led by Leif Eriksson made landfall in what is now Maine. Viking ships also likely visited areas farther north, such as Greenland and Nova Scotia. But despite this brief brush with the West, for many centuries Europeans remained ignorant of the existence of the continents that later came to be known as the Americas and

of their inhabitants. Most Europeans believed that the Atlantic Ocean stretched until it lapped the shores of India—or more likely, dropped into a limitless void.

That misconception was dispelled on October 12, 1492, when Italian sea captain Christopher Columbus landed on what are now the islands of the Bahamas. Mistakenly believing that he had reached India, Columbus called the tribal inhabitants he met there Indians. He made more trips in the following years, landing in other Caribbean islands. Other explorers, many financed by ambitious European monarchs, soon followed.

Christopher Columbus prepares to embark on his historic voyage to what he hoped would be Asia, but turned out to be America.

COLONIZATION OF THE NEW WORLD

Europeans quickly realized that what they had found was not India but an entirely different continent. Many European governments, wealthy individuals, and newly formed business enterprises sent explorers, traders, and soldiers to explore and exploit what are today known as North, Central, and South America. Europeans began to claim American lands on behalf of their rulers.

Colonists and Native Americans face off in one of the many conflicts that characterized the European colonization of America.

By the early 1600s many Europeans viewed the New World as a place of religious freedom as well as economic opportunity. America was so far from Europe that kings, popes, and other rulers would not be able to tell the colonists how to live, what religion to practice, or what they may or may not say. And, unlike Europe—where every square foot was already known, mapped, and belonged to someone—America seemed (at least to the new arrivals) to offer limitless unclaimed spaces. The poorest colonist in America could, it appeared, claim a piece of land as his own property. Such opportunity prompted many Europeans, who sought either religious freedom or an improvement in economic circumstances, to immigrate to the New World, where they founded settlements.

Some colonists, like Rhode Island's founder, Roger Williams, befriended America's indigenous peoples and defended their rights; many other colonists simply seized natives' lands and fought any who resisted. Conflict between Europeans and Native Americans grew from mutual misunderstanding as well as from competition for natural resources. Native Americans did not understand at first that millions more Europeans lived on the other side of the ocean, that these new arrivals intended to stay, and that many more would be coming. For their part, European immigrants usually failed to see Native Americans as having legitimate claims to the land they inhabited. At any rate, even tribes that were actively hostile to the colonists could not, in the long run, defend themselves against Europeans armed with superior weapons.

Not every new arrival in the Americas went there willingly. In 1619 a Dutch ship delivered the first African slaves to the British colony of Jamestown, Virginia. It was the beginning of the slave trade in America. In the following years Dutch, Spanish, and English traders purchased thousands, then millions, of captured Africans—some of whom had been kidnapped by rival tribes in Africa. Slave traders shipped these captives to the West Indies or to the American mainland. Those who survived the trip, made in wretched and inhuman conditions, were sold as property and used as manual labor, mostly on plantations that grew tobacco and cotton. While a few blacks were allowed to purchase their freedom or were freed outright by their owners, most lived out their lives in slavery.

THIRTEEN BRITISH COLONIES IGNITE A REVOLUTION

By the 1770s England had established thirteen separate, largely self-governing colonies in North America. Connecticut, Delaware, Georgia, Maine, Maryland, Massachusetts, New Hampshire, New Jersey, New York, Pennsylvania, North Carolina, South Carolina, and Virginia all possessed their own governors and legislatures. Most of the colonies had local laws permitting freedom of religion, freedom of public assembly, and the rights of

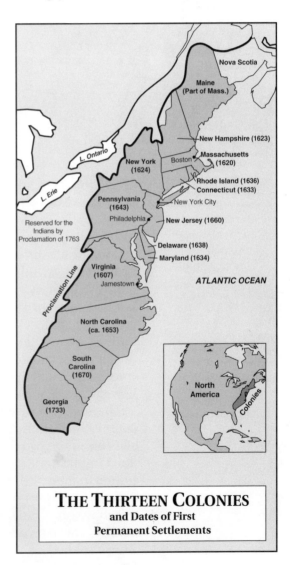

THE THIRTEEN COLONIES
and Dates of First
Permanent Settlements

George Washington takes command of the American army at Cambridge, Massachusetts, on July 2, 1775.

colonists to govern themselves in many matters of business and public life through their local elected governments.

Although the thirteen colonies were officially British, almost two hundred years spent far from direct control by the king had fostered a sense of independence that the colonists jealously guarded. When King George III of England tried to impose taxes that the colonists considered unfair, his majesty's colonial subjects refused to pay them. The colonists insisted that they should have more say in deciding how they were ruled.

The king, supported by Parliament, decided to remind the colonists who was really in charge. England declared that self-rule in the two most rebellious colonies, Massachusetts and Virginia, was over. Local legislatures would not be permitted to meet; British generals were put in charge of both colonies. The port of Boston was closed so that no food or dry goods could be shipped in. In an additional affront, some colonial homeowners were forced to provide housing for British soldiers.

In response to this treatment, which the colonists considered tyranny, they began to store guns and ammunition and to create an army, in case fighting broke out. In 1775 fighting did erupt in Massachusetts between the amateur colonial soldiers and the professional British troops. Realizing that they needed to speak with one voice, colonists also sent representatives to Philadelphia to form a leadership group known as the Continental Congress. This body appointed an American soldier and plantation owner, George Washington, as the general of its combined forces, the Continental Army. Although the colonists had yet to declare it, the long Revolutionary War had begun.

THE DECLARATION OF INDEPENDENCE

At first the war was fought simply to force Britain to give the colonies more local self-rule and to end the hated taxes. But as the fighting dragged on, American colonists increasingly saw that America must separate itself from Britain and form an entirely new nation. On July 4, 1776, the Continental Congress voted to adopt the Declaration of Independence. This

Delegates sign the Declaration of Independence, the document that formally severed the tie between the colonies and Britain.

historic document announced the birth of the new nation and explained to King George why the colonies were breaking away from England. Thomas Jefferson, an idealistic young Virginian, led a group of Continental Congress members in authoring the declaration. Even today, Jefferson's words still inspire and define the dream of liberty within law for many people around the globe.

As Jefferson wrote in the declaration,

> We hold these truths to be self-evident, that all men are created equal; that they are endowed by their Creator with certain unalienable rights; that among these are life, liberty and the pursuit of happiness; that to secure these rights, governments are instituted among men, deriving their just powers from the consent of the governed.[3]

THE IMPACT OF THE DECLARATION

The document created a wave of disquiet among European leaders. Historian Leslie Lipon writes that the

> impact of the Declaration in creating a new state [arose from the fact that] this was the earliest occasion when a colony [of any European empire] rebelled and asserted its own right to self-government and nation-statehood. . . . The effect on those Europeans who opposed the traditional order was overwhelming.[4]

European leaders understood that the Declaration of Independence could also have an immense impact on the rest of the world. British prime minister Lord North said at the time, "If America should grow into a separate empire, it must cause a revolution in the political system of the world, and if Europe did not support Britain now, it would one day find itself ruled by America."[5] Distinguished American historian Henry Steele Commager more recently wrote that the declaration raised the question "Would the American revolution turn into a world war?"[6] No such global conflict ensued, but historians agreed that the Declaration of Independence and the American Revolution together likely served as the inspiration for later revolutions in France, South America, and elsewhere. As Lipon concludes, "No continent has stayed immune from the consequences."[7]

THE REVOLUTIONARY WAR

From 1775 to 1781, the Continental Army fought a difficult war to win American independence. Most American soldiers were volunteers who suffered from numerous disadvantages compared to their British foes. They were poorly paid; short on food, uniforms, and arms; and were almost untrained. As a result, the well-trained and well-armed British army captured the colonies of New York, Rhode Island, and Delaware and won many other battles. But America's army endured and even won some surprise victories by using guerrilla tactics it had learned from Native Americans.

Finally—with important aid from France in the form of soldiers, supplies, and naval support—colonial forces defeated the British army in 1781. British troops went home, and British control over America's laws, shipping, and economy ended. The thirteen colonies became free, independent states joined in a loose partnership under an agreement called the Articles of Confederation. This partnership proved short-lived, however.

THE STATES CREATE A STRONG CENTRAL GOVERNMENT

In 1788 the newly formed states agreed that they needed a strong national government to decide issues of common concern, including currency, defense, diplomacy, and interstate commerce. Once again, the leaders who had declared America's independence and won its war with England met in Philadelphia, this time to hold the Constitutional Convention. These men organized the thirteen American states under a constitution, a set of fundamental laws designed to define the relationship between the people, the states, and their national government.

The U.S. Constitution established an American government that was republican—that is, the country would be governed by representatives who spoke for the people and did their bidding rather than by rulers who told the people what to do. The new government was also democratic, which, to America's founders, meant that each adult white male would have the right to vote for his representatives, either directly or indirectly. Just as important, the government was federal, which meant that it shared power with the states.

Such a government had never been tried before. In the past, rulers had usually inherited power or taken it by force.

Although democracies had existed a few times before in history, participation had been limited to very small groups of wealthy voters. And earlier democracies had always eventually become politically unstable, internally corrupt, or had been conquered by more tightly controlled, centrally ruled nations. Despite these earlier failures, America's founders believed that free people could govern themselves successfully. In choosing a democratic republic for its form of government, then, the United States of America was undertaking a grand—and some thought dangerous—experiment. At the close of the Constitutional Convention, Ben Franklin, one of the founders, was asked, "Well, Doctor, what have we got: a republic or a monarchy?" The wise old statesman replied, "A republic—if you can keep it."[8]

THE IROQUOIS LEAGUE INSPIRES BEN FRANKLIN

For uncounted generations—perhaps beginning as early as the 1200s—six Native American tribes were united in a confederation known as the Iroquois League. This league was governed by a constitution known as the Kainerkowa, or "the Great Law of Peace," whose features were described in 114 wampum pictograms. A supreme council of fifty male "peace chiefs" included tribal representation that was permanently fixed at fourteen members of the Onondaga tribe, ten of the Cayuga, nine of the Oneida, nine of the Mohawk, and eight of Seneca. Tribal clan mothers nominated the male representatives, who were appointed for life but could be recalled for poor performance. Different parts of the intertribal council functioned, in effect, as executive, legislative, and judiciary branches. The Iroquois constitution explicitly provided strict rules of procedure to provide checks and balances.

Benjamin Franklin, one of America's founders, was familiar with the Iroquois and strongly approved of many features of their league. As early as 1751, Franklin advocated a similar system for the American colonies. In Bruce E. Johansen's *Forgotten Founders,* Franklin's comments appear in the form of a letter to a friend: "It would be a very strange thing if Six [Indian] Nations . . . should be capable of forming such an Union and be able to execute it in such a manner, as that it has subsisted Ages, and appears indissoluble, yet a like Union should be impracticable for ten or a dozen English colonies."

By 1797 nine states had ratified the Constitution—enough to bring it into force as the basis for a new, unified nation. The four remaining states agreed to ratification after the United States adopted the Bill of Rights. This document, which took the form of ten amendments, or additions, to the new Constitution, guaranteed fundamental rights such as the freedom of speech, worship, and assembly; freedom of the press; the right to security in one's home; and the right to a fair and speedy trial.

A crowd in New York City cheers as George Washington is inaugurated as the first president of the United States in 1789.

Even then, however, America was far from being a perfect democracy. Several of the original states permitted blacks to be bought and sold as slaves. Women in the new United States lacked voting rights. It would be nearly eighty years before slavery ended, and longer still before women would participate fully in choosing their government's leaders.

AMERICA'S FIRST PRESIDENT

The new nation elected the commander of its victorious Continental Army, George Washington, as its first president. In his first inaugural address, Washington spoke of the new nation as the American experiment that would determine whether mankind could preserve what he called (in a nod to Native American tradition) "the sacred fire of liberty."[9] Washington

FIRST IN WAR, FIRST IN PEACE: GEORGE WASHINGTON

George Washington was loved and admired by virtually all Americans of his day. Standing six feet two inches tall and perhaps the Continental Army's finest horseman, Washington's sheer physical power and grace impressed his contemporaries. Even more impressive was his powerful character: He conveyed a passionate nature, checked only by immense self-control. Washington said little, but his words carried tremendous weight.

Largely self-educated, Washington won his battle stripes in the French and Indian Wars of the 1750s. During the Revolutionary War, General Washington never commanded more than fifteen thousand troops at any one time. But he kept America's army together and led it to eventual victory. After the war, Washington resigned his commission and retired to private life, returning to politics five years later to preside over the Constitutional Convention.

Washington served two terms as America's first president from 1789 to 1796. He did not especially want the job, but he accepted it to promote U.S. political unity. His first inaugural address, published in *George Washington in His Own Words*, includes this statement: "The preservation of the sacred fire of liberty, and the destiny of the republican model of government, are justly considered as deeply, perhaps as finally staked, on the experiment entrusted to the hands of the American people."

served two terms, then retired to private life on his plantation and turned the government over to his elected successor, John Adams.

Again, this voluntary change in leadership was unprecedented: Leaders of most countries left power only when they died or were overthrown. As the popular former commander of the army, Washington probably could have rallied his troops and held power by force, remaining America's leader for the rest of his life. His voluntary surrender of power therefore astonished much of the world.

By leaving office peacefully and voluntarily, Washington began an American tradition: the orderly transfer of governmental authority. He also reinforced America's tradition of civilian control of the military. These traditions helped ensure that America's government remained stable and unified, even during times of war, economic calamity, or other periods when political passions ran high. Plenty of tests of America's unity lay ahead, though.

WESTWARD EXPANSION

The new nation grew rapidly as settlers pushed beyond the thirteen original states into what, at the time, was considered the West: the territory lying between these first states and the Mississippi River. Growth accelerated when America's third president, Thomas Jefferson, agreed to purchase the Louisiana Territory from France for $15 million. This single transaction added 58 million acres to America's holdings, doubling the size of the new nation with some of the richest land in the world at the bargain price of three cents per acre! In 1846 the United States made a treaty with Britain to acquire part of the Oregon Territory, which includes the modern-day states of Oregon, Washington, and Idaho.

Other land acquisitions by the United States were less peaceful. Americans fought bloody wars with Mexico and with Native Americans to add Texas, Florida, California, Utah, Arizona, and New Mexico to America's territory. In making all of these purchases and conquests, America added people, settlements, and cultures of French, Hispanic, Mexican, and Native American origins to its national mix.

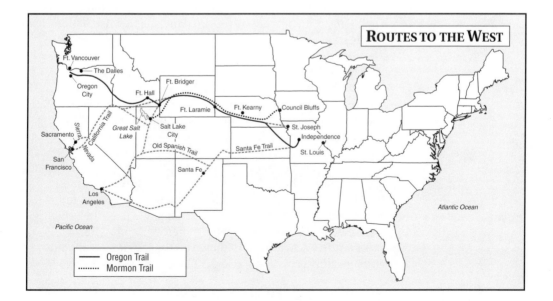

The discovery of gold in the California Territory in 1847 spurred another massive westward migration. Gold hunters swelled California's population from fifteen thousand people in 1848 to one hundred thousand just two years later. Other resources drew hundreds of thousands of trappers, cowboys, farmers, settlers, and tradesmen into the central and western regions of the country. They came on foot and on horseback; by boat, wagon, and railroad. While some failed in their endeavors and left, many more stayed. They created farms and ranches in the wilderness and built towns with homes, schools, and churches.

These pioneers fought inhospitable climates and rugged terrain. Private citizens and the U.S. Army alike fought a long-running war against the native peoples whose tradi-

 ## SACAGAWEA GUIDES LEWIS AND CLARK

After making the Louisiana Purchase, President Thomas Jefferson ordered a survey of the continent. In 1804 he sent two army captains, Meriwether Lewis and William Clark, to find the source of the great Missouri River and learn other geographical facts about the unexplored North American wilderness. Lewis and Clark began their trip from St. Louis, which was then at the edge of the settled territory. Over a period of several years, they trekked to the Pacific Ocean and back. Their long, difficult journey provided invaluable information for the trappers, settlers, and pioneers who followed them into the new land over the next eighty years.

Lewis and Clark said they could not have made their successful trip without the help of Sacagawea, a courageous and resourceful young Shoshone tribeswoman who served as their guide. Sacagawea, whose name means "Bird Woman," led Lewis and Clark over the Rocky Mountains and floated down the Columbia River with them, all the way to the Pacific Ocean, carrying her baby with her the entire time. Sacagawea was overjoyed when, along the way, the exploring party found her Shoshone tribe, from which she had been separated for many years. It turned out that her brother was the tribe's chief, and Lewis and Clark were treated as heroes for bringing his sister home. Sacagawea is depicted on the U.S. dollar coin that entered circulation in the year 2000.

tional homelands they had taken. Many settlers and Native Americans died in the struggle.

Despite many obstacles, by 1860 the U.S. flag flew over cities, towns, and settlements from the Atlantic to the Pacific Oceans. The question of America's survival as a unified nation still had to be settled, however.

Pioneers in the mid-1800s cross the Great Plains on their long journey west.

"LET FREEDOM RING": EXPANDING THE FRONTIERS OF LIBERTY

As settlers moved west and newly formed territories applied to join the Union, America was forced to confront the ugly contradiction between its democratic ideals and the persistence of slavery in the South. Conflict between Northern and Southern states over slavery grew sharper. The disagreements led to heated political battles in Congress; legal battles in the courts; passionate arguments in newspapers, homes, and churches; and outbreaks of violence in places from Kansas to Harpers Ferry, Virginia.

In 1860 the political conflict over slavery climaxed when Abraham Lincoln was elected president of the United States. His party, the Republicans, stood for the total abolition of slavery in America. "A house divided against itself cannot stand," Lincoln had said earlier. "This government cannot endure permanently, half slave and half free. . . . I do not expect the house to fall. . . . It will become all one thing, or all the other."[10]

Once in office, Lincoln and the Republicans in Congress refused to allow slavery in newly admitted states. In response, eleven Southern states announced that they were seceding from the Union on the theory that each state had voluntarily joined the United States and could voluntarily leave. Leaders of Virginia, Mississippi, Florida, Alabama, Georgia, Louisiana, Texas, North and South Carolina, Arkansas, and Tennessee met and declared themselves a part of a new nation, which they called the Confederate States of America. Convinced that President Lincoln would use military force to keep the United States together, Confederate troops attacked the Northern-held Fort Sumter in South Carolina. The long and bloody Civil War was under way.

In the beginning, many Americans saw the Civil War as a conflict simply to determine whether the South should be allowed to leave the Union. For five years, the North and the South fought each other. Armies waged terrible battles in and around the farms, villages, and cities of the South, the West, and the border states. Soldiers on both sides died by the tens of thousands.

THE EMANCIPATION PROCLAMATION AND UNION VICTORY

As the war dragged on, Lincoln realized that he had to address the slavery issue, which had become foremost in the minds of most Americans. In 1863 he issued the Emancipation Proclamation, declaring all slaves in the Confederacy free by his order as president and commander in chief. By 1865 Union armies, supported by greater resources, had systematically destroyed or captured the South's food stocks, railroads, and supplies. The Confederate army, starving and surrounded by superior forces, surrendered that year.

Lincoln's proclamation and the Union victory in the Civil War were insufficient, by themselves, to guarantee equal rights for all Americans. True equality came slowly; it took more than another century of hard work and sacrifice by many people, black and white, to address in a meaningful way the legacies and traditions of slavery, racial discrimination, and hatred.

The abuses of slavery constitute the dark side of American history.

GLORIOUS TRAGEDY: THE PRESIDENCY OF ABRAHAM LINCOLN

Abraham Lincoln, America's sixteenth president, saw the country through its greatest crisis, the Civil War, and saved America from destruction. Both loved and hated in his own time, Lincoln's greatness is universally acknowledged today. As the author of the Emancipation Proclamation, which abolished slavery, Lincoln was a powerful moral as well as political force.

Born in a log cabin to poor parents, "Abe" Lincoln became a (mostly self-taught) lawyer before running for Congress in 1846. As president, Lincoln created the North's successful war strategy of constant all-points advances, and he hired and fired generals until he found some who could put his plans into action. Tall and gaunt, his soberly distinguished public image masked a witty yet depression-prone personality. At the close of the war, Lincoln counseled forgiveness for the South. However, only days later, he was shot and killed by John Wilkes Booth, a resentful Southerner.

One of Lincoln's wartime speeches, the 1863 Gettysburg Address, has achieved worldwide immortality. This classic expression of America's political ideals reads, in part,

> Fourscore and seven years ago, our fathers brought forth upon this continent a new nation, conceived in liberty and dedicated to the proposition that all men are created equal. Now we are engaged in a great civil war testing whether that nation, or any nation so conceived and so dedicated, can long endure. . . . We here highly resolve that . . . this nation under God shall have a new birth of freedom, and that government of the people, by the people, for the people shall not perish from the earth.

Abraham Lincoln, the sixteenth U.S. president.

As the nineteenth century drew to a close, equal justice remained elusive. Native Americans, even though they were born in the United States, still lacked citizenship. Women still lacked voting rights. Worse yet, some American leaders, supported by Supreme Court rulings, blunted the effect of the constitutional amendments passed in the 1860s and 1870s to guarantee equal rights to former slaves. For decades, blacks in both the North and the South endured racial segregation and discrimination. That meant inferior public schools and housing, fewer job and educational opportunities, and—too often—beatings, murders, and legal oppression.

AMERICA'S ROLE IN THE WORLD

As the twentieth century dawned, the United States turned from internal concerns to asserting itself as a world power. From 1900 to 1930, successive American presidents sent the U.S. Marines to invade Western nations such as Cuba, Haiti, Nicaragua, and others to support U.S. interests. One president during this era, Theodore Roosevelt, said his foreign policy was to "speak softly and carry a big stick"—meaning, use friendly diplomacy whenever possible, but always be ready to back those words with military power. A real test of America as a military power was coming.

When general war broke out in Europe in 1914, President Woodrow Wilson tried at first to keep America out of the conflict. When German submarines began sinking American ships, Wilson decided freedom was threatened globally. "The world must be made safe for democracy,"[11] Wilson said. In 1916 he led Congress to declare war and sent American troops to France, where they fought alongside French, British, and Italian allies. Americans played a decisive role in the defeat of the Central Powers: Germany, Turkey, and the Austro-Hungarian Empire.

After the war the idealistic Wilson tried to win generous peace terms for the defeated nations, but his allies sought vengeance. Wilson also promoted a new worldwide alliance of countries called the League of Nations, whose members pledged to defend each other from aggressive foreign powers. Many European countries joined the league, but the U.S. Senate—reflecting most Americans' wishes to avoid foreign commitments—refused to ratify the treaty.

THE JAZZ AGE AND THE GREAT DEPRESSION

In the years following World War I, Americans again turned their attention to domestic affairs. During the 1920s the country enjoyed an expanding economy driven by the widespread use of new products like commercial radio sets and mass production of automobiles and other consumer goods. A booming stock market—in which even modest investments grew into fortunes—added to America's sense of well-being. America's prosperity fueled vigorous new ways of living. Young people in their twenties took the leading role in popular culture for the first time, creating new music like jazz and the blues, new media like "talking pictures" (movies with synchronized soundtracks), new dances, and freer rules of courtship and social behavior. For many city dwellers and the middle and upper classes, the era seemed like a nonstop party. "Life is just one grand sweet song, so start the music,"[12] quipped Ronald Reagan, who was a high-school senior in 1928.

The Ford delivery department in 1925, filled with new automobiles. Mass production of cars contributed to the booming economy in the 1920s.

The party ended with a stock market crash in 1929. Many investors lost everything practically overnight. Within four years tens of thousands of banks, businesses, and even schools closed. Unable to repay loans because of low crop prices, many thousands of farmers lost their farms. One-third of all U.S. workers lost their jobs. America was caught in a worldwide economic depression: production, purchases, incomes, and property values all plummeted.

During the 1930s America focused on recovering from the Great Depression. Urged on by President Franklin D. Roosevelt, Congress passed many new laws that authorized the creation of programs and agencies to stimulate business and put Americans back to work. Other new laws regulated banks, currency, and stocks more closely to help prevent future economic collapses. Roosevelt's program—known as the New Deal—was controversial because the federal government had never before exercised so much power to regulate business and the economy.

The New Deal did not entirely end the depression, but it did put many people back to work and restored America's self-confidence. "The only thing we have to fear is fear itself,"[13] President Roosevelt asserted. Echoing George Washington's original characterization of America as an experiment in liberty, Roosevelt also said, "The country demands bold, persistent experimentation. It is common sense to take a method and try it. If one thing fails, admit it frankly and try another. But above all, try something."[14]

America Enters World War II

America's economy was still weak from the Great Depression when President Roosevelt recognized a growing menace abroad: power-hungry dictatorships in Japan, Italy, and Germany. These nations began invading and conquering their neighbors in the mid-1930s. Roosevelt hoped he could help negotiate peaceful settlements of the resulting conflicts, but he advocated increased U.S. military readiness in case diplomacy failed. Through a program known as Lend-Lease, America provided weapons, supplies, and encouragement to countries under attack. "We must be the great arsenal of democracy,"[15] Roosevelt said.

At first most Americans wanted nothing to do with foreign problems, especially wars. They supported a neutral "stay home" policy in the belief that America could remain isolated from the rest of the world. Even though U.S. citizens knew foreign dictatorships oppressed and murdered their neighbors and even their own citizens, Americans still hoped they could stay out of the bloody, faraway conflicts.

U.S. hopes for neutrality suddenly ended on December 7, 1941, when Japanese warplanes mounted a surprise attack on America's military base at Pearl Harbor, Hawaii. Two days after the attack, Germany and Italy also declared war on the United States. Like it or not, Americans were plunged into global conflict once again, and Americans united in their determination to achieve total victory. Shocked by news of atrocities committed by Nazis against conquered peoples, Americans came to view the war as more than just a battle to defend the United States; the conflict also became a crusade to protect human rights around the world.

The war raged for almost four more years, prompting development of new weapons such as radar, jet planes, and rockets. Overpowered by massive Allied forces, first Italy and then Germany surrendered. Then, in August 1945, the United States attacked Japan with the most terrible weapons of all: two atomic bombs, which had been secretly developed by scientists working under U.S. military authority. Days later, Japan capitulated.

Smoke billows from the damaged U.S.S. Arizona *at Pearl Harbor after the surprise Japanese attack on December 7, 1941.*

World War II ended in 1945 after the United States dropped two atomic bombs on Japan.

HOPES FOR GLOBAL HARMONY

As peace returned, Americans found that World War II had fundamentally changed America's status and position in the world. Once economically weak, U.S. industries were soon humming with activity as houses were built and companies produced new cars, telephones, and other goods for millions of returning veterans. Untouched by bombing or invasion and vastly strengthened by wartime production, America's industries in 1946 accounted for fully half of the world's total economic output. Once isolationist and militarily outmatched by other nations, the United States was now deeply—and, it seemed, permanently—involved in foreign affairs with large numbers of troops stationed in Asia and Europe; and until 1949 the United States was the only nation possessing nuclear weapons.

In the immediate postwar years, Allied leaders were determined to use these advantages to build new international systems of laws and economics that would preserve world peace while promoting freedom and prosperity. The Allies helped create prosperous democracies in Japan, Italy, and

Dr. Martin Luther King Jr. gives a speech at a civil rights demonstration in Atlanta, Georgia. King fought tirelessly to achieve equal rights for black Americans.

Germany. America led the way in creating a new organization called the United Nations (UN), in which countries could work together for justice and human rights. Former first lady Eleanor Roosevelt chaired the international commission that created the UN and served as America's first ambassador to that body, which was headquartered in New York City. The United States also created and supported many global economic assistance programs and agencies, most notably the Marshall Plan, which spent billions of dollars to revive the shattered, starving nations of Europe.

THE CIVIL RIGHTS MOVEMENT

Domestically, America's attention turned once again to civil rights for its black citizens. Many Americans were recognizing that the evils of racism that had been vanquished abroad should not be tolerated at home. President Harry S Truman ordered the desegregation of the U.S. military in 1946. The U.S. Supreme Court ruled against racial segregation in schools in 1954, and President Dwight D. Eisenhower sent federal troops to Southern states to enforce that ruling.

MARTIN LUTHER KING JR.: A VOICE FOR JUSTICE

Martin Luther King Jr., the son and grandson of respected Atlanta preachers, grew up in the segregated South of the 1920s and 1930s. "M. L.," as his family called him, became an ordained minister as well, taking his first pulpit in Montgomery, Alabama. In 1954 King became embroiled in a racial conflict that erupted when a black seamstress named Rosa Parks refused to give her bus seat to a white passenger. Montgomery's blacks organized a boycott against the busline and drafted King as their leader. Inspired by Mahatma Gandhi's principles of nonviolent resistance, King sustained the boycott for over a year despite lawsuits, official harassment, and even the terrorist bombing of King's own home. Similar boycotts sprang up nationwide, and King's group triumphed when the U.S. Supreme Court declared that their action was legal. The Court ordered the city to integrate equal bus seating for blacks and whites. King found himself at the forefront of African Americans' national battle for equal rights.

King and other black ministers founded the Southern Christian Leadership Conference (SCLC) in 1957. This organization used what King called creative nonviolence—marches, protests, sit-ins, and the like—to protest America's widespread racist conditions, inequalities, and discrimination. After moving to Atlanta in 1963, King traveled the nation and led dramatic protests in places like Birmingham, Alabama, where peaceful and lawful activities by African Americans provoked harsh police attacks. Heavy news coverage of the protests and police actions shocked white Americans with the horrific state of race relations. City by city and state by state, King and the SCLC forced the South's white racist establishment to yield.

King's finest moment came on August 28, 1963, when he stood at the Lincoln Memorial and delivered his famous "I Have a Dream" speech, defining in soaring rhetoric a moving vision of a color-blind America that would "live out the true meaning of its creed . . . that all men are created equal." Over two hundred thousand Americans, including many whites, attended and cheered. Congress passed the Civil Rights Act in 1964, and King won the Nobel Peace Prize for his work. More peaceful protests followed in Selma, Alabama, provoking more stormy confrontations, more news coverage—on television this time—more political shock, and finally more landmark legislation in the shape of the 1965 Voting Rights Act. King spent his final years working for economic equality before being gunned down by an assassin in 1968 at age thirty-nine.

A great civil rights movement led by Martin Luther King Jr. and others in the 1950s and 1960s inspired Congress to pass more powerful voting and civil rights acts to ensure social and political equality for black Americans. Today many Americans can still recite parts of King's electrifying 1963 speech:

> I have a dream that one day this nation will rise up and live out the meaning of its creed: "We hold these truths to be self-evident, that all men are created equal.". . . I have a dream that my four little children will one day live in a land where they will not be judged by the color of their skin, but by the content of their character. . . . From every mountainside, let freedom ring.[16]

Progress on civil rights came at a horrific cost, including violence against peaceful demonstrators, race riots, and the assassination of black leaders such as King himself in 1968. But gradually African Americans moved into schools, jobs, and neighborhoods that had previously been reserved for whites. In the 1960s blacks were elected to the U.S. Senate and big city mayorships and were appointed to their first U.S. Cabinet positions. In the 1970s and 1980s, a growing percentage of African Americans earned college educations and achieved middle-class economic status. Although some racial discrimination and economic disparity persists and disagreement over how to eliminate economic inequality simmers, the country continues to seek genuine equality for all of its people.

THE COLD WAR: GLOBAL COMPETITION BETWEEN EAST AND WEST

While Americans sought racial equality at home, the nation's leaders attempted to achieve similar benefits for the citizens of other nations as well. Yet organizations and programs such as the United Nations and the Marshall Plan could not, by themselves, ensure peace and freedom. Following World War II, the Soviet Union kept its troops in countries liberated from Nazi domination. Occupied by Soviet forces, Eastern Europe became a network of Communist-ruled police states. In addition, Russia began encouraging, intimidating and forcing other countries around the world to adopt pro-Soviet governments or even to submit to direct Russian control. Virtually overnight, America's former ally became its greatest rival for international influence.

President Truman believed that the free world must avoid repeating the passivity of the 1930s, which had helped spark World War II. Truman committed the United States to resisting Soviet expansion. The United States and its Western European allies formed the North Atlantic Treaty Organization (NATO) as a mutual self-defense group against Soviet intimidation and potential invasion.

America's cold war policy succeeded in defending democratic values in Western Europe and Japan. U.S. diplomatic backing was also crucial for the creation of a new democratic state, Israel, in 1948. However, in countries like Taiwan, Haiti, the Congo, and Guatemala, the United States provided support for dictators simply because these leaders opposed communism.

This worldwide U.S.–Soviet conflict lasted forty years. It was called the cold war because it was often fought indirectly through political, diplomatic, and military maneuvering rather than direct confrontation between the two nuclear superpowers. Sometimes the conflict led to small surrogate wars: Each side's allies fought in far-flung places, ranging from the Sinai Desert in the Middle East to Africa, El Salvador, and Nicaragua. On other occasions, the cold war involved American or Soviet troops in combat: The United States sent troops to Korea in the 1950s and to Vietnam in the 1960s, and the Soviet Union poured its forces into Afganistan in the 1980s. In 1962 the cold war even threatened to escalate into a possible nuclear exchange as President John F. Kennedy and Soviet premier Nikita Khrushchev confronted each other over the USSR's placement of nuclear missiles in Cuba.

The cold war mainly meant a nonstop arms race. East and West built enormous military forces and nuclear arsenals to intimidate each other and prepare for the possibility of all-out war. Ironically, knowing that a nuclear exchange could destroy all human civilization, both sides embraced a military strategy of mutual-assured destruction—the belief that nuclear war's utter finality would itself prevent leaders from waging such a horrendous conflict. Meanwhile, a generation of American schoolchildren remembered frightening classroom drills—ducking under desks or taking shelter in hallways—in preparation for a nuclear war that, fortunately, never came.

AMERICANS FOUGHT THE COLD WAR AT HOME, TOO

The effect of the cold war on American domestic politics was as far-reaching as its impact on foreign policy. In the 1940s and 1950s, America suffered through a "red scare" or period of anti-Communist hysteria. The conversion of China, the world's most populated nation, to communism in 1949 only poured fuel on the fire, as did the unexpectedly early achievement of nuclear capability by the Soviet Union that same year.

Propelled by such events, national leaders rushed to demonstrate their patriotism. Both of America's major political parties supported ill-advised moves such as outlawing the U.S. Communist Party and setting up Loyalty Boards to review the political views of government workers. The U.S. House of Representatives created an Un-American Activities Committee to investigate charges—mostly groundless—of Communist propaganda in American broadcast media and motion pictures. Many radio, television, and movie executives voluntarily created blacklists—some open, some secret—to bar Communists or former Communists from working, while turning much of America's popular culture into flag-waving propaganda. Most notoriously, Wisconsin senator Joseph McCarthy charged that hundreds, perhaps thousands, of known Communist double agents were employed in the U.S. State Department and other federal agencies and organizations. Most of McCarthy's charges were false, sensationalistic, and undocumented, but for several years many Americans seemed ready to believe that an insidious Communist influence lurked around every corner.

In the 1960s and 1970s, cold war politics gave way to domestic culture clashes. A new feminist movement demanded equal rights, opportunity, and pay for women in government, law, schools, and the workplace. The black civil rights movement split into several factions, some embracing radical militancy while others remained committed to nonviolence and a religious perspective. Meanwhile, other American minorities such as Latinos and Native Americans organized and demanded to be included as equal partners in American society.

Such developments challenged the country's traditional ways of thinking and, at times, its power structure. Results were mixed: America benefited from an enlightened political atmosphere in which new laws were passed protecting the civil rights of African Americans, the environment, and women's rights. Yet the clash of views led to a series of tragedies, including a series of race riots in cities from Los Angeles to Washington, D.C.; a riot at the 1968 Democratic National Convention in Chicago; and four fatalities when U.S. National Guard troops fired on peaceful antiwar protesters at Kent State University in Ohio. Even more shocking, the era was marred by assassinations: President John F. Kennedy in 1963 and civil rights leader Martin Luther King Jr. and Senator Robert Kennedy in 1968. Government investigations determined that each murder was committed by individual, probably deranged, gunmen.

CESAR CHAVEZ: THE VOICE OF FARMWORKERS

One of the twentieth century's greatest labor leaders, Cesar Chavez, showed that organizing a successful labor movement could become a noble human rights crusade. Chavez was ten years old when, in 1939, his family lost the farm they owned because they were unable to pay the taxes. The family moved from Arizona to California to become migrant farmworkers. By age sixteen, Chavez had dropped out of school to earn money for his family, working on a carrot farm for two dollars a day. Latino leaders of the Community Service Organization (CSO) in San Jose, California, were determined to organize their people to fight the whites-only segregation that was common at the time and work for better conditions for all workers. In the early 1950s, Chavez became a political activist, registering Latino citizens to vote. By 1958 he had become the director of the CSO.

Chavez left the CSO in 1962 to follow his dream of organizing farmworkers into a union—something many said could not be done since these workers were often on the move and spoke little or no English. Chavez sank his life savings—twelve hundred dollars—into creating the National Farm Workers Association (NFWA) and driving all over California's Central Valley to recruit members. An admirer of Gandhi and Martin Luther King Jr., Chavez led his followers on nonviolent protest marches and held sing-ins to call attention to the workers' conditions. Farm owners threatened to fire any workers who joined the NFWA, but by 1965 the organization counted seventeen hundred members when it joined with Filipino grape pickers in a strike against the growers. Chavez staged a twenty-five-day hunger strike and called on Americans to boycott grapes. The boycott eventually spread across the United States, and by 1970 the growers agreed to raise wages and sign contracts.

It was the first of many strikes, boycotts, and protests over the next twenty-three years, leading to a difficult but steady improvement in conditions for migrant farmworkers. Despite having a family of his own, union president Chavez took only ten dollars a week as salary. His dedication and idealism earned him the admiration and love not only of Latinos but also of Americans everywhere. At the time Chavez died in 1993, he knew that the union still had a long way to go before conditions for migrant workers would be truly fair. Some fifty thousand people attended his funeral. In 1994 Chavez was posthumously awarded the Presidential Medal of Freedom.

America's domestic turmoil climaxed in 1973–1974 with a constitutional crisis. Newspaper and government investigations showed that President Richard Nixon and members of his administration had systematically broken many laws by using both government agencies and private political agents to spy on, smear, and illegally investigate their political opponents. The Nixon administration then committed further abuses in an attempt to cover up the first set of crimes. Facing certain impeachment and conviction, President Nixon resigned from office in August 1974. The new president, Gerald R. Ford, reassured Americans that "our long national nightmare is over. Our Constitution works."[17]

RECESSION AND RECOVERY

With the end of the military draft in 1973 and the end of the Vietnam War in 1975, America's domestic political tensions eased even while its economic woes mounted. Skyrocketing fuel prices, mounting inflation, and high unemployment combined to create the worst domestic economy since the Great Depression. Those Americans who did have jobs labored under

Ronald Reagan's accomplishments during his two terms as president include lowering taxes and cutting inflation.

Sandra Day O'Connor: America's First Female Supreme Court Justice

Sandra Day O'Connor's story symbolizes the plight, and rise, of American women during the twentieth century. After graduating third in her class at Stanford Law School, O'Connor faced the grim realities of gender discrimination: No law firm was willing to hire her as an attorney. The best offer she received, in fact, was to work as a legal secretary. Failing to find an appropriate position, given her training, she opened a private practice near Phoenix, Arizona, where she lived with her husband. Taking time off for motherhood, she raised three sons. Once back at work, she became active in state politics, running for office and winning election to the state senate.

O'Connor later became a judge; she earned a reputation for being tough but fair while serving on the state appeals court. In 1981 President Ronald Reagan nominated O'Connor to serve on the U.S. Supreme Court, the highest honor—and toughest job—in the American legal system. O'Connor accepted and was easily confirmed by the Senate. She is known as a conservative but open-minded jurist who often provides the crucial swing vote on a variety of issues before the Court. On a Court that frequently divides along sharp ideological lines, O'Connor's fellow justices—including Ruth Bader Ginsberg, appointed in 1993—praise her for being able to find common ground and pragmatic solutions that a majority can support. Speaking of her pioneering status, O'Connor made this wise and witty remark, which was quoted in an April 1999 profile in *Biography* magazine: "Even more important than being the first, is not being the last."

the highest tax burden in the country's history. Likewise, America's traditional heavy industries—steel, oil, and automobiles—lost money and market shares to tough overseas competitors. The future seemed both uncertain and troubling.

Americans elected Ronald Reagan president in 1980 on the strength of his promises to cut taxes, reduce government spending, conquer inflation, and restore prosperity. Reagan also pledged to reassert America's leadership in foreign affairs. Reagan succeeded in cutting taxes and inflation as he had promised, although he did not achieve his goal of reducing government spending, which meant that budget deficits rose sharply during his two terms in office. But after undergoing a very steep recession, America embarked on its longest economic boom ever. The next two presidents, George Bush and Bill Clinton, continued the policies of seeking to hold down interest rates, shrink the size of government, and reduce regulation of America's businesses. Aided by falling oil prices and a new surge of technological development—especially in the field of computers—the U.S. economy created tens of millions of new jobs between 1980 and 1999.

VICTORY FOR THE WEST

The cold war finally ended in 1991, when Soviet leaders realized that their tightly controlled economy could not compete with the accelerating technological and communications revolutions of free-market economies. The Soviets also admitted that they could not afford to maintain and continually modernize their military forces.

As the cold war died down and the Soviet Union began pulling its forces from Eastern Europe, newly freed countries like Poland and Czechoslovakia immediately formed democratic governments. In 1991 the Soviet Union itself dissolved into fifteen separate nations, including Russia, the Ukraine, Georgia, and Latvia. Some became democracies; several ended (or at least softened) totalitarian control. America befriended these former Soviet states, supplying multibillion-dollar loans, food, and technical assistance in hopes of promoting the development and success of friendly democracies.

During the 1990s the United States tried to lead the way in helping promote peace in the world, with mixed results. For example, an American-led coalition of nations (including Russia) successfully forced Iraq to withdraw its troops from Kuwait. But efforts to end ethnic violence in the Balkan nations of Yugoslavia and Bosnia forced American troops into the unwanted role of international police. Many Americans questioned their nation's self-appointed role as the world's policeman.

THE AMERICAN EXPERIMENT CONTINUES

Within their own nation, Americans believe the original American idea remains valid and adaptable to any and all new circumstances. Beyond America's borders, its citizens are redefining their international role in a changing world, still guided by the founders' original beliefs: that free and equal citizens can be self-ruled through government "of the people, by the people, and for the people," that each person has the right to pursue his or her unique vision of happiness, and that individuals can best determine their own destinies. As the twenty-first century began, Americans continued the quest they began in 1776 to let freedom ring, even as they questioned how best to accomplish that goal.

3

AN ECONOMIC SUPERPOWER: THE CREATIVE ENERGIES OF FREE PEOPLE

Supplied with abundant natural resources and invigorated by a dynamic free-enterprise system, the people of the United States have built the globe's strongest and most varied economy. In fact, America's economy is over twice the size of the world's second largest economy, Japan's. Among major industrialized nations, Americans create the fastest rate of economic growth. They spark the greatest amount of innovation in key fields, as measured by patents granted annually (124,146 in 1997, over 50 percent more than the next leading nation). Americans employ the highest percentage of the available workforce. Individual U.S. citizens and private companies make most economic decisions for themselves, although government plays a vital role in the nation's economy. Through taxing and spending, government provides regulation, infrastructure, and social benefits to many citizens.

Yet for all its strengths, the American economy also faces several long-term challenges. These include inequalities in education, incomes, and job opportunities; environmental pollution; large trade deficits; inadequate medical insurance for many workers; and conversion of many companies from defense-based economies to civilian applications.

The dynamic nature of the U.S. economy is revealed by any number of measures. America's total yearly output of goods and services, the gross domestic product, is the world's largest: an estimated $8 trillion in 1997. Americans account for just 5 percent of the world's population, yet the country's 136 million workers produce approximately one-fourth of the world's total goods and services. America enjoys additional key strengths in fields such as aerospace, telecommunications, and biomedical research. "The world's eight largest hitech companies are all U.S.–based,"[18] the *New York Times* reported in 1999. Other important U.S. industries include petroleum, agriculture, steel, automobiles, chemicals, electronics, food processing, consumer goods, lumber, and mining. Often called "the Breadbasket of the World," America's farmers lead all other countries in food production and exports.

PRIVATE CITIZENS TAKE THE INITIATIVE

The U.S. economy is called a free-enterprise or market-oriented system. This means that private citizens and individual businesses decide most economic issues for themselves. Economists Robert L. McCan and William H. Peterson say the shape of America's economy is "constantly evolving out of the choices and decisions made by millions of citizens who play multiple, often overlapping roles as consumers, producers, investors and voters."[19] For example, individual citizens, rather than government officials, decide for themselves where and how much education they get, what jobs to take, and how much to ask or

THE BREADBASKET OF THE WORLD

The nation's founders believed that farming created honest, self-reliant people. Such citizens, they thought, could best succeed in democratic self-government. For many years this romantic attitude about farming dominated much of the country's cultural and political dialogue. When America was founded, most of its people lived and worked on farms. Today only 2 percent of Americans do so (fewer than 3 million out of 270 million people). Despite their dwindling numbers, American farmers provide food to the United States and much of the world. Close to 1 million acres of the United States are devoted to agriculture, raising nearly 600 million farm animals and producing $216 billion in agricultural income. The country includes over 2 million farms (down from 5.7 million in 1900). The average American farm today comprises 461 acres, with well over $500,000 in assets (real estate, machinery, buildings, seed, and livestock); it grosses about $100,000 per year. Farm productivity tripled between 1960 and 1990. Major U.S. crops include corn, wheat, cotton, potatoes, tobacco, cattle, and swine.

The United States produces more of the world's food crops than any other country.

accept for their work. Private companies decide whether and when to open or close factories, invest in research and development, create new products, and hire or fire workers. As opposed to Socialist or Communist systems in which a nation's government owns key industries and farmland, in the United States individuals own these assets, sometimes individually and sometimes through buying and selling shares in corporations on the stock market. Rather than producing the materials it uses, the U.S. government buys most of what it needs from privately owned companies.

Within a free-enterprise system, individual citizens—not the government—must largely act on their own initiative. It takes vision, courage, and hard work to invent a new product, launch a new business, or pioneer a brand-new industry. Someone has to create the ideas, do the research, and shoulder the risk. But the opportunity to take those risks, and perhaps reap the rewards of success, is a major reason why America's economy is so attractive to people around the world. Victor Swan, a Lebanese immigrant who owns a highly successful furniture factory in Los Angeles, explains: "People always say, 'you foreigners work too hard.' But it's the foreigner like me who comes here to work. When you're an outsider, you try harder. And the more you try, the better chance you'll succeed."[20]

Sometimes, participants in the American economy may get advice and low-cost loans from government sources or private institutions such as banks. On a regular basis, the U.S. government, by guaranteeing that loans will be repaid, sees to it that new businesses can be nurtured. A relatively recent innovation in the American economy that is rapidly being emulated elsewhere in the world is venture capitalism—a form of private investment that provides startup funds for promising new companies. But in each case, individual citizens must also risk their own time, money, and effort, especially at the beginning of a new career or a new business.

Since there is no guarantee of success in a free-enterprise system, individuals and companies in America must be willing to try, fail, learn from their mistakes, and try again. This need for resilience applies to everyone in the United States. It applies to a recent immigrant whose family scrapes together enough money to start a small restaurant, hotel, or cleaning business. It applies equally to a long-established

 ## Henry Ford Puts America on Wheels

Henry Ford, the founder of the Ford Motor Company, pioneered mass production of the automobile. In the 1890s, before Ford came along, cars were considered unreliable and expensive toys for rich people; most people used horses, horse-drawn carriages, or trolleys to get around in cities; they used trains or ships to travel longer distances. Ford's development of the moving assembly line enabled his factory to build Model T cars so cheaply that millions of working people could afford to buy these "Tin Lizzies."

From 1908 through the 1920s, the Ford Motor Company built half the cars sold in the United States. Ford's innovation permanently transformed much of America. Highways and gas stations created to accomodate cars came to dominate the landscape. Design uniformity, mass production, and mass marketing took over the American economy. Automobiles even profoundly changed American social customs—from dating to commuting to family recreation.

manufacturing giant whose multimillion-dollar investment results in a new design for cars or computers. Many of the most successful people and companies in the United States experienced one or more failures, even bankruptcies, before achieving ultimate success. As one of America's great business pioneers, automobile manufacturer Henry Ford, expressed it, "Failure is just the opportunity to start again, more intelligently."[21]

 ## "ONE GIANT LEAP FOR MANKIND"

On July 20, 1969, U.S. astronaut Neil Armstrong emerged from his spacecraft, climbed down a ladder, and stepped onto the surface of the Moon. He thus became the first human being in history to set foot on a celestial body besides Earth. "That's one small step for a man," Armstrong said, "and one giant leap for mankind."

Unlike past explorers and adventurers—ranging from Columbus to Charles Lindbergh—Armstrong was not a solo performer or the leader of a small group. His mission resulted from a twelve-year crash program of American space exploration. Prompted by the Soviet Union's success in launching history's first artificial satellite and first astronaut, the United States responded by setting a goal that, by 1970, it would land a man safely on the Moon and return him to Earth.

This goal symbolized the U.S. public's optimistic belief that Americans can accomplish anything they set their minds to. The American government spent billions of dollars to fund the mission. The U.S. National Aeronautics and Space Administration (NASA) oversaw private industry's development of rockets, spacecraft, tracking and communications devices, and space suits. NASA also supervised the U.S. military's training of astronauts and ground-based support teams. America remains the only nation to have placed human beings on the Moon, but the lunar body does not belong to the United States. Neil Armstrong and his fellow astronaut Buzz Aldrin left behind a plaque that proclaims: "We came in peace for all mankind."

U.S. astronaut Buzz Aldrin on the moon.

GOVERNMENT PROVIDES ECONOMIC SUPPORT

The United States is called a mixed economy, which means that private ownership controls most goods and services, but government still "plays a central role," as President Bill Clinton explains.

> The federal government has the [critical responsibility] of creating the framework in which our economy can grow. . . . [This includes] reducing the deficit, bringing interest rates down, holding inflation in check, restraining bad business practices, expanding opportunities for world trade, supporting research and technology, and increasing educational opportunity.[22]

America's federal government alone spends about $1.6 trillion every year, the single largest budget of any U.S. entity. The money spent by America's federal, state, and local governments comes in part from taxes. Public spending helps create jobs and stimulates production of certain goods and services. It also provides broad structural support for all U.S. industries and direct individual help to millions of American citizens. Specifically, public funds are used to build, operate, and maintain what is called infrastructure: schools, highways, national and state parks, railroads, seaports, airports, canals, and navigational systems, to name just a few examples. Spending on infrastructure is just one way the U.S. government participates in the American economy.

GOVERNMENT REGULATION TO ENSURE SAFETY AND FAIRNESS

Regulation is another way America's government creates a framework for a sound economy. Government agencies strictly regulate banks, currency, and trading on the stock market. In addition, by determining key interest rates, the federal government plays an important role in seeing that money can be borrowed by individuals and corporations for use in building homes, starting new businesses, or purchasing improved equipment. Besides managing some aspects of the economy directly, the government also indirectly participates in Americans' economic activity. For example, the government sets standards for fair hiring, worker safety, product safety, and the quality of goods and services ranging from air travel to milk. The government sets import and export rules

The freeways, highways, and roads Americans travel on are supported by government funds.

and imposes duties (import taxes) on selected goods. During extreme emergencies such as wartime or an economic crisis, the government may even take direct control of wages, prices, production, and every vital industrial activity.

Americans continually debate the question of how much government involvement is best for the economy. Because their well-being is tied to how well the nation's economy performs, citizens frequently vote for a candidate based on that person's economic plans. Some leaders favor more regulation and taxation in order to ensure fair competition, redistribute wealth, and help needy citizens. "We believe in only the government we need, but we insist on all the government we need," New York's governor Mario Cuomo once said in a speech to fellow members of the Democratic Party.

> We believe, as Democrats, that . . . the most affluent democracy in American history . . . ought to be able to help the middle class in its struggle, ought to be able to find work for all who can do it, room at the table, shelter for the homeless, care for the elderly and infirm, hope for the destitute.[23]

Other U.S. leaders favor fewer social programs, less regulation, and lower taxes. They believe that a relatively unfettered free market provides the best opportunities for citizens to prosper and for businesses to grow. This school of thought also asserts that ever-growing government programs and ever-increasing regulations can mean decreasing individual liberty. "Never forget that any government big enough to give you everything you want, is strong enough to take it all away,"[24] Senator Barry Goldwater once charged.

Recent U.S. presidents such as George Bush and Bill Clinton have taken a centrist approach, mixing some government regulation and intervention with support for free trade, low interest rates, and other policies that promote stable economic growth. Depending on the most recent election results, the government's involvement in America's economy shifts continually.

CHALLENGES AND PROBLEMS

While the free-enterprise system has fostered U.S. technological leadership and dynamic growth, this very dynamism also creates instability and uncertainty for companies and employees alike. With less government regulation than any other industrial nation, U.S. firms can—and frequently do—suddenly open and close, grow and shrink, get bought or sold, or suddenly shift their location or structure. This means that individual American workers may need to retrain and reposition themselves for the market's changing demands on their skills and talents.

Workers also face the ever-present possibility of being laid off or transferred to a new job, sometimes with little or no advance notice, even when the economy seems to be strong. This is particularly true as America's economy becomes more and more dominated by companies whose products are constantly changing. America's technology-driven boom "has carried with it hidden costs, including a dramatic increase in temporary-help jobs, widening income disparity and generally shorter tenure and longer periods of unemployment for most workers [in high-tech-driven markets],"[25] according to a 1999 report by the Ford Foundation and the Economic Policy Institute.

The term *income disparity* means that U.S. workers tend to be divided into two very different groups. Better-educated workers and those with highly developed technical skills tend to enjoy many job opportunities, high salaries, regular pay raises, medical insurance, and other benefits. Less-educated, less-skilled workers often miss out on such rewards. Accordingly, the quality of U.S. public education remains an ongoing concern, especially when surveys taken year after year show that many American schoolchildren rank low in basic skills when compared to their counterparts in other industrialized nations.

The vital relationship between education and earning power in the United States is clearly reflected by the fact that, on average, Americans with high-school diplomas earn about twenty-two thousand dollars annually, while those with college degrees average at least thirty-eight thousand dollars per year. From the federal government down to the local school boards, debate rages on how to encourage children to complete at least twelve years of school and how to make those years as productive and meaningful as possible. "We know today that every year of job training or further education beyond high school—whenever it occurs in life—increases a worker's future earnings anywhere from 6 to 12 percent," President Bill Clinton states. "If we want Americans to earn more, we need to help them learn more."[26]

Workers with advanced education and technical skills are likely to get jobs with higher salaries and better benefits than their less-educated counterparts.

As America enters the twenty-first century, the need for the nation's schools to provide students with increasingly sophisticated job skills is apparent. Of the total labor pool of 136 million, more than 97 million will be working in service industries where employees must be skilled at tasks such as word processing and complex operations with data. Only about 25 million Americans currently work in production-type jobs, but even there workers find that familiarity with computers and other high-tech equipment is vital. In a very real sense, government action affects Americans' abilities to respond to the changing needs of their workplaces and to earn their living.

OTHER CHALLENGES FOR THE U.S. ECONOMY

The very size of U.S. corporations, while ensuring their market power and ample resources to perform research and development of new products, can also lead to problems like stagnation or unfair domination of the market. For example, America's auto industry, which originally included dozens of small manufacturers in the early 1900s, had become dominated by three major manufacturers by midcentury. During the 1950s and 1960s, the "Big Three" automakers (Ford, General Motors, and Chrysler) became spoiled by years of easy sales of large, heavy cars. When fuel prices tripled in 1973, these companies failed to respond quickly to consumer demand for smaller, more fuel-efficient cars. Sales fell dramatically, leading to massive employee layoffs. The hardships were felt throughout the U.S. economy, but particularly in regions where the auto industry had supplied many of the jobs. By 1980 unemployment as high as 25 percent was recorded in Flint, Michigan, for example, where the vast majority of workers depended on the fortunes of General Motors. U.S. automakers did not fully regain their competitive position until they introduced a new generation of cars in the late 1980s.

Another long-term challenge for America's economy is insufficient investment in economic infrastructure. For example, tens of thousands of bridges are in disrepair across the country; some are dangerous. Many cities and suburbs need more roads and highways and better water supplies to meet the needs of growing populations. Although it is usually cheaper to address aging infrastructure early rather than waiting until a crisis occurs, U.S. citizens often resist paying the higher taxes or higher prices required for aggressive solutions. The federal government has responded by making some tax money available for improved infrastructure.

TOWARD A MORE GLOBAL ECONOMY

During the latter part of the twentieth century, American businesses increasingly sought to grow by improving their ability to compete in other countries. Once seen as secondary to the domestic market, the global economy now drives growth for most American manufacturers and for much of U.S. agriculture. For example, Coca-Cola, rather than remaining satisfied with sales that grew only as the U.S. population grew, took aggressive aim at sales in foreign countries, which now account for over 50 percent of its annual revenue. This heavy reliance on foreign sales is increasingly typical for American manufacturing firms, which average anywhere from 40 to 60 percent of their sales outside the United States.

Americans believe that their free-enterprise economy works to the extent that it unleashes the creative energies of free people to follow their own vision and determine their own destinies. Private initiatives from individuals and groups, supported by targeted government spending and careful regulation, do yield impressive results—from the world's most prosperous economy and the planet's most productive agriculture industry to technological innovations like the Internet. Even though many major challenges remain, Americans face their problems with confidence that their economic system can overcome almost any obstacle. As the growing global economy makes the world's nations increasingly interdependent, the United States continues to generate unprecedented wealth, opportunity, and innovation for an ever-growing number of its citizens and business partners at home and abroad.

"FROM SEA TO SHINING SEA": AMERICA'S LAND AND LANDMARKS

Geographically diverse and rich in natural resources, the United States is a land of extremes. Topography ranges from the vast flat expanses of the great Central Plains to the rugged peaks of the western Rocky Mountains. Soaring ice-capped mountains, broad glaciers, and river valleys dominate Alaska while the Hawaiian Islands feature lush jungle vegetation and volcanic peaks. The sheer size and variety of U.S. geography offers "an ecological extravagance that disappeared from other continents long ago but that borders on hyperbole in North America,"[27] comments one nature expert.

America's geographic extremes include its longest river, the Missouri, which flows for 2,540 miles (4,090 kilometers). The United States and Canada share the world's second largest lake, Lake Superior—all 31,820 square miles of it (82,414 kilometers). California's Yosemite National Park is home to one of the world's highest waterfalls, the Ribbon, which cascades from a height of 1,612 feet (491 meters). America's highest point, Mount McKinley in Alaska, reaches 20,320 feet (6,198 meters). The highest point in the forty-eight contiguous states is California's Mount Whitney at 14,495 feet (4,418 meters). The lowest point is Death Valley, California, at 282 feet (86 meters) below sea level.

At 3,615,292 square miles (9,363,563 square kilometers), the United States is the world's third largest nation in terms of area, accounting for 6.2 percent of the globe's total land mass. Its comparative size is half that of Russia, slightly larger than China, half the size of South America, and about two and a half times the size of Western Europe. Spanning six

National parks such as Yosemite in California (pictured) preserve some of the most beautiful natural areas in the United States and offer exceptional outdoor recreation.

time zones, the United States stretches from Maine in the east to Alaska's Attu Island in the west.

America's mainland includes the whole midsection of North America. Beginning at the Atlantic shore, the nation reaches 2,807 miles (4,517 kilometers) across the continent to the Pacific Ocean. The United States enjoys the world's longest unfortified national boundary with Canada to the north (1,538 miles or 2,475 kilometers) and an equally impressive transcontinental border with Mexico to the south (1,933 miles or 3,111 kilometers). Beyond the continent, America also includes the Hawaiian Islands, located in the Pacific Ocean some 1,000 miles away from America's west coast.

Seven major geographic regions compose the U.S. mainland: the Appalachian Mountains; the coastal lowlands; the Great Plains; the Ozark-Ouachita Mountains; the Rocky Mountains; the western plateaus, basins, and ranges; and the Pacific ranges and lowlands. Partly overlapping and partly corresponding to the nation's geographic divisions are an equal number of major cultural and economic zones. Defining such human boundaries (as opposed to topographical demarcations) is necessarily an arbitrary exercise; but as a nation of nations, America does include distinctive regional characteristics. In his book *The Nine Nations of North America,* author Joel Garreau identified several major cultural-economic zones within America itself: New England, the Foundry, Dixie, the Breadbasket, the Empty Quarter, Ectopia, and MexAmerica. (Garreau also identified North America's two remaining regions as French-speaking Canada and the combination of South Florida and the islands of the Caribbean. He marked off New York City and Washington, D.C., as unique exceptions dominated by their own local cultures rather than fitting into any regional scheme.)

THE ROCKY, HILLY NORTHEAST: NEW ENGLAND

The northern sector of the Appalachian Mountains and the coastal lowlands are home to the New England region, which includes the states of Maine, New Hampshire, Vermont, Massachusetts, Rhode Island, and Connecticut. The northern sector's older, gently sloped White Mountains and Green Mountains give way to forested, rocky-soiled hills and then to the wilderness-like New York Adirondack Mountains, which feature many beautiful lakes. New England offers much beautiful scenery but few natural resources. For example, suitable farmland is scarce in Vermont's and Maine's rocky, hilly countryside. The region also lacks oil, major mineral deposits, and the sorts of rivers that could be dammed to generate hydroelectric power.

New England's intellectual capital is Boston, a city that is home to dozens of colleges and universities, including Harvard, the Massachusetts Institute of Technology, and Boston University. The region's high quotient of brainpower drives a postindustrial, information-based economy whose computer business was booming long before the rest of the nation began scrambling to catch up.

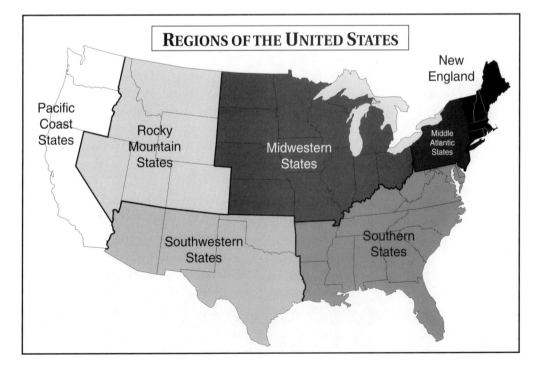

REGIONS OF THE UNITED STATES

The region's celebrated independent streak shows up in the way New Englanders buck development trends and forgo certain kinds of corporate profits in order to zealously conserve their beautiful woodland and coastal ecologies. For example, citizens of the region strongly resisted sprawling commercial development and the building of nuclear power plants long before doing so became popular elsewhere in the country. Today New Englanders continue to resist development that could be environmentally damaging, such as offshore oil drilling. Interestingly, despite the high value New Englanders place on individuality, compared to the rest of America, local government in New England tends to take more taxes per capita but also to provide more services—such as Boston's extensive rapid transit system and the region's extensive public housing.

THE MID-ATLANTIC: NERVE CENTER OF BANKING, POLITICS, AND COMMUNICATION

The Mid-Atlantic officially includes the states of New York, New Jersey, and Pennyslvania, although many Americans think of this region more generally as including the entire

The spectacular Niagara Falls in New York is one of the mid-Atlantic states' most famous landmarks.

The capitol building in Washington, D.C., the seat of the United States government.

New York–Washington corridor—that is, the sprawling, densely populated megalopolis that stretches from America's largest city, New York, in the north, to the nation's capital, Washington, D.C., in the south. In between lie many other teeming cities, including Philadelphia, Trenton, Elizabeth, and Newark.

Geographically, the region offers hundreds of miles of sandy seashores; moving westward, these give way to grassy rolling hills and eventually rise up to foothills and finally to low mountains like the Alleghenies. A marked feature of the region is the extensive chain of islands, rivers, inlets, and deepwater harbors that make the Mid-Atlantic a leading center for international trade. Outstanding natural landmarks include Niagara Falls, located on the New York–Canadian border, while human-made landmarks include the spires of New York City itself and the huge tunnels and bridges connecting New York to New Jersey.

The Mid-Atlantic is the most densely populated geographic region in America with over 80 percent of its people living in urban areas. The region is also a leading U.S. manufacturing center, producing a wide variety of goods—including garments, computers, photographic equipment, and pharmaceuticals—as well as serving as America's center of printing and publishing. America's headquarters for communications, banking, and publishing is found in New York, which also boasts the region's busiest harbor.

The Mid-Atlantic region also is home to the "industry" of the U.S. federal government, one of America's major employers. Washington, D.C.'s distinctive landmarks include the White House (home of the president of the United States) and the dome of the U.S. Capitol, where members of Congress meet.

THE MIDWEST AND CENTRAL PLAINS: THE BREADBASKET AND THE FOUNDRY

The American Midwest is marked by the Central Plains and the five Great Lakes: Erie, Huron, Michigan, Ontario, and Superior, which make up the world's largest freshwater lakes. This region's rich soil deposits and plentiful rain support much of America's robust agricultural industry. While no longer as large as they once were, the region's automobile, steel, and other heavy industries employ a sizable number of America's workers.

The Central Plains, covering the middle quarter of the United States, are known as the Heartland. The flatland is so vast that observers can see the horizon's straight line twenty to thirty miles away. Moving westward, these plains slowly incline to higher elevations and receive progressively less rainfall. "From an airplane, the middle of North America looks like an endless grid of backgrounds and superhighways, surrounding mosaics of irregular fields and growing crops," states one observer.

> Superimposed on this agricultural checkerboard are squiggles of forests along rivers and jagged patches of untamed pastures. . . . [Once] the landscape amounted to just prairie, sky, and wind. The sky and wind are still there, but most of the prairie has been turned over to crops.[28]

Dominated in terms of acreage by farms (even though most of its citizens are not farmers), the Heartland accounts for 18 percent of the world's wheat exports. American agribusiness makes its chief living from sophisticated deals on various world markets. The Midwest is also home to America's heavy industries. Building on abundant natural resources such as iron ore, lumber, coal, and water for transportation, Americans established smokestack industries such as steel, oil, coal, and automobile manufacturing in gritty midwestern towns and cities like Chicago, Illinois; Gary, Indiana; Flint, Michigan; Cleveland, Ohio; and Detroit, Michigan. Detroit still claims to be the auto capital of the world, but today most midwestern states have been forced to diversify their economies to remain competitive in the new global market. Ohio, for example, remains a leading industrial state by making such products as rubber in Akron, jet engines in Cincinnati, and steel in Youngstown; yet the state has augmented its economy by promoting $9.7 billion in annual tourist trade to such landmarks as Cincinnati's Rock and Roll Hall of Fame and the Indian burial grounds at Mound City Group National Monument.

Dixie: The Old South Becomes the New South

The southeastern region of the United States, ranging from Florida to eastern Texas and as far north as Virginia and mid-Missouri, is nicknamed "Dixie." (Nobody knows for certain where this nickname originated.) The South includes an incredibly diverse mix of geography, including mountain

 ## The Mighty Mississippi

At 2,340 miles, the Mississippi is not America's longest river, but it does stand as the most important one in terms of America's history—and it cuts the biggest swath through American life and folklore. The river begins in northwestern Minnesota, heading north at first, then doubling back upon itself. It twists and winds its way lazily southward, passing half a dozen states on each riverbank and forming the natural boundary between America's eastern and midwestern regions. The river finally flows into the Gulf of Mexico. Along the way, its drainage basin covers nearly 1.25 million square miles of America's richest farmland.

Also fondly called "the Big Muddy" and "Old Man River," the Mississippi provided a route for French and Spanish explorers in America's early days. By the 1800s, steamboats found it a perfect waterway for transportation and commercial shipping. American author Mark Twain prominently featured the river in two of his greatest books—*Life on the Mississippi* and *Huckleberry Finn.* Today the Mississippi River still carries some 60 percent of the total freight transported on U.S. inland waterways: about 460 million short tons float down Old Man River each year.

ranges such as Virginia's Blue Ridge and Tennessee's Smokies (both named for the haze that often hangs over them), sandy beaches and islands such as those associated with the Carolinas and Florida, and piney hills in Arkansas and eastern Texas. From naturalist David Middleton's point of view,

> What ties together this most ecologically varied ecoregion is the pulse of migration that annually swings north and then south along the broad reach of the Atlantic. Caught between the mountains and the shore, the Atlantic Coast is a natural corridor for animals traveling with the seasons. In fact, migration never ceases along this path.[29]

As a cultural-economic zone, the South comprises the eleven states of the old Confederacy along with all or parts of several border states. Agriculture was traditionally the major southern industry and remains important to the New South; key crops include cotton, tomatoes, corn, and tobacco. Although Dixie's economy includes the enduring

The Kennedy Space Center at Cape Canaveral, Florida, is the site of space shuttle and manned rocket launches.

poverty of rural shacks in South Carolina, it is also defined by oil, light industry, and commercial fishing; and the nation's space shuttles and manned rockets are launched from the Kennedy Space Center at Cape Canaveral, Florida.

Despite the fact that agriculture is vital to the South's livelihood, the region is home to large cities such as Atlanta, Georgia, and Miami, Florida. Atlanta, comparing itself to other southern cities with histories of troubled race relations, calls itself "the City Too Busy to Hate." Featuring skyscrapers, excellent rapid transit systems, and one of America's three busiest airports, Atlanta is as sophisticated as any northern metropolis. Miami, although also a major southern city, has a feel completely different from Atlanta. Often described as the cultural capital of the Latin American world, Miami is famed for its lively Cuban-dominated music and nightclub scene.

Once home to slavery and long dominated by its aftermath, the South has overcome much of its racist history and reluctance to integrate African Americans into its society—although citizens of color are quick to point out that much progress remains to be made. Still, in many southern cities, majorities of blacks and whites regularly elect African Americans as mayors, police chiefs, and city council members. Since the 1970s the South has also boasted America's best-integrated school populations.

The American West: The Empty Quarter and MexAmerica

Geographic extremes are easy to find in the American West, which combines snowcapped mountain peaks and flat, fertile grasslands; forbidding deserts and inviting beaches; spectacular geological rock formations without a living thing in sight; and giant trees that are the world's largest living organisms. Socially and economically, the West is also America's wealthiest and fastest-growing region, supporting the greatest ethnic population mixture and a broad range of industry, ranging from oil, mining, and agriculture to high technology, entertainment, and aerospace.

The Great Plains, with its seemingly endless seas of grass, runs through states like Montana and the Dakotas. These plains are used for cattle grazing, but they also contain fertile farmland. California, Nevada, Utah, Arizona, and New Mexico boast vast stretches of drylands, deserts, and wastelands—strange

ARIZONA'S SPECTACULAR GRAND CANYON

In a landscape famed for giant-sized features, the mile-deep, 217-mile-long, and nine-mile-wide Grand Canyon is the biggest of them all. Carved by winds and the Colorado River over millions of years, the canyon's epic size and beauty stagger all who see it. Even upon personally viewing this immense landmark, a visitor cannot realize its full size until something provides a sense of scale. Perhaps the visitor rides a mule down steep paths to the canyon's floor. Looking up, the visitor finally realizes just how dizzyingly tall those rock walls really are— taller than the tallest skyscraper ever built by human hands.

Size is not the Grand Canyon's only amazing quality. Its range of colors changes each hour as the shifting sunlight and clouds play on the multiple hues, shadings, and rock striations. Located in the southwestern state of Arizona, the canyon is the chief feature of the 1,875-square-mile Grand Canyon National Park.

The overwhelming natural beauty of Arizona's Grand Canyon makes it a popular tourist attraction.

and spectacular geological formations of wind-carved mesas, rock bridges and natural stone arches. Among these great natural wonders stand the sculpted sentinels of Monument Valley and the world's largest gorge, the Grand Canyon.

Equally impressive is the Sierra Nevada mountain chain, which runs through central California and parts of Nevada.

According to one researcher,

> The Sierra Nevada Mountains boast many superlative qualities. For example, they are the longest range with the highest mountain, Mt. Whitney, in the lower 48 United States. Home to the southernmost glaciers in North America, this range has received the most snowfall in a season: 86 feet on Donner pass during the winter of 1983. The Sierras boast two marvels: 8,240-foot-deep King's Canyon, which is several thousand feet deeper than the Grand Canyon, and 2,425-foot-tall Yosemite Falls, the third highest waterfall in the world. . . . And on [the Sierra's] slopes grow the largest living thing ever to grace the Earth—larger than a blue whale, larger than any dinosaur, and larger even than the largest redwood—the giant sequoia tree.[30]

Author Joel Garreau describes the West as "the Empty Quarter," noting that much of the West is characterized by vast distances of untouched, uninhabited territory between towns, cities, and settlements. Most of these undeveloped lands are controlled and owned by the U.S. government. The Empty Quarter sustains the lowest population in terms of people per square mile of any major U.S. region. Nevertheless, it contains abundant mineral resources—gold, silver, uranium, petroleum, and zinc, among many others. This region's colorful local culture and economy blend the cowboy heritage and open spaces of the Old West with the get-rich-quick mining and gambling ethic of cities like Denver and Las Vegas. Denver businesses control half of America's gold production, and Las Vegas—America's casino capital—was the nation's fastest-growing city during the late 1990s.

Much of the West, however, is anything but empty. The Sunbelt—including California, Nevada, Colorado, and New Mexico—drew America's greatest regional population growth during the last decades of the twentieth century. In part, the West's growth has come at the expense of other regions of the country. But the West has also attracted many immigrants from abroad. People from Mexico, other Latin American countries, and many Asian nations now are part of the West's culture.

Latinos are the largest minority in a growing number of southwestern towns and cities, and the majority in some.

Hispanic influences on the West's regional culture range from the wide availability and popularity of Mexican food to the fact that the highest-rated radio stations in cities like Los Angeles feature the Spanish language. In fact, the prominence of Latino culture is one of the reasons Garreau dubbed part of the Sunbelt "MexAmerica." Yet America's greatest number of ethnic Asians also live in the West and have also had a major impact on its culture, from individual achievements in science and technology to the broad popularity of martial arts and physical disciplines like tai chi.

THE PACIFIC NORTHWEST: GREENS AND DEVELOPERS

America's Pacific Northwest is known for the beauty of its thick forests, vast glaciers and permanent snowfields, powerful rivers, and dramatic coastline. The region also includes the nation's most recently active volcano, Washington's Mount St. Helens, which last erupted in 1980. The Pacific Northwest holds relatively few mineral deposits but is rich in timber, supplying about one-third of America's lumber, especially softwoods such as Douglas firs, hemlocks, ponderosas, and white pines. The region includes vast coastal mountain ranges forested with giant redwoods reaching heights of three hundred feet. These ranges sometimes meet the sea in dramatic sheer cliffs, possibly rimmed with a tiny sliver of beach. Other Pacific coastlines offer broader beaches leading to gentle sandy plains and rolling hills. Large bays cut far inland at Puget Sound, the Columbia River Bay, and the San Francisco Bay.

Culturally, the region embraces an ecology-friendly philosophy of clean industry and a social tolerance. Garreau calls the region "Ectopia" to convey its determination to preserve its natural beauty. "The Pacific Northwest, politically, economically, and socially, is operating on some fundamentally different assumptions from its neighbors,"[31] Garreau assserts. *New Scientist* magazine notes, for example, that

> Oregonians are an outdoor people, and are willing to follow their love of nature to its political conclusions in support for environmental policies at the ballot box....
> As former Governor Tom McCall put it, "No one in his right mind wants to be caught voting against a big reason why most people live here in the first place."[32]

Sequoia National Park in California includes forests of giant sequoia trees.

Paradoxically, commercial logging and fishing remain major industries in the Pacific Northwest, and the goals of loggers and fishermen often conflict with the goals of preservationists who resist uncontrolled logging and exploitation of fisheries. Accordingly, even those who make their livings in these industries tend to depict themselves as being environmentally friendly. For example, northwestern logging companies point to their reforesting and old-growth policies that, they claim, help protect forestlands.

A Landscape of Freedom

America's sprawling open spaces have exercised a powerful influence on the American character and imagination. A favorite traditional song speaks of "spacious skies" and "amber waves of grain," suggesting both the largely untrammeled wilderness that would permit political freedom and the material abundance that could support that freedom. From ocean to ocean, the United States remains a broad and mighty land, rich in geographical diversity and natural resources that support the lives of a dynamic people.

5

AMERICA NOW:
GOVERNMENT OF, BY, AND
FOR A DIVERSE PEOPLE

On any given day some Americans can be found climbing mountains, hiking, or camping in U.S. wilderness tracts while others are breaking ground in similar tracts to build new homes, factories, and shopping centers. Still other Americans might be applying for jobs in the companies that plan to occupy those new developments. Yet others may be organizing a protest against urban sprawl or its environmental impact. Similarly, on any given day some Americans will be found participating in religious activities while others will be found debating the merits and scope of allowable religious activity within the public schools.

To decide among all these competing goals and agendas, Americans seek constructive compromises through their elected government representatives and in the courts. The U.S. government is based in Washington, D.C., but through the employees of its various agencies, it reaches into the remotest territories of America.

The three branches of government—executive, legislative, and judicial—are designed to work together to serve the needs of all citizens and residents of the United States. How well the U.S. government functions depends on a number of factors. These include the shifting opinions and desires of the public, the willingness of America's elected representatives to work together, and the quality of ideas and leadership provided by elected and appointed officials—from the president down to members of the local school board.

The U.S. Constitution divides power among the three governmental branches to create a system of checks and balances. This arrangement prevents any one branch from becoming too powerful and dominating the others, a condition that—the Constitution's authors feared—might lead the government to dominate, rather than serve, the people. One example of constitutional checks and balances is found in the fact that Congress's power to pass laws stands in opposition to the president's power to sign or veto legislation. The Supreme Court's power to decide whether a particular law accords with the Constitution itself provides yet another potential check on Congress's lawmaking authority. Similarly, the president's authority as commander in chief of the armed forces is checked by Congress's sole power to declare war.

The ultimate check on the power of the executive and judicial branches of government is impeachment, a constitutionally prescribed remedy whereby Congress can indict, try, and possibly remove from office federal public servants who have abused their positions of trust. Two presidents and scores of federal judges have been impeached over the course of the nation's history, but Americans are reluctant to impeach a president or other high-ranking federal officer because the disruption to the nation's political life can be severe. Nevertheless, the method remains available to help ensure that public officials can be removed should they fail to keep faith with the country's laws.

The U.S. capital Washington, D.C., where all three branches of the government— executive, legislative, and judicial—work together in a system of checks and balances.

THE LEGISLATIVE BRANCH: CONGRESS

The U.S. government's legislative branch is embodied in Congress, an elected body totaling 535 lawmakers—435 in the House of Representatives and 100 in the Senate. The main function of Congress is to enact laws that affect all Americans. Congress determines such vital issues as how much of their income Americans will pay in taxes, how those taxes will be spent, the minimum wage an American business must pay its workers, and a wide array of other concerns. The House and Senate make such decisions by voting on separate bills, sometimes after lengthy debate. Members of Congress meet with their constituents both in Washington and back in their home states and districts to learn what voters think about issues facing Congress.

Because a diverse population with widely varying interests elects the members of Congress, disagreements in Congress are inevitable. Often the result of such disagreements is a compromise, with the opposing parties reaching an agreement through mutual concession. At other times, a stalemate occurs and the business of Congress stalls until someone either changes positions or Congress as a whole decides to set an issue aside and take up other concerns instead. For example, Congress has agreed, in theory, that the nation's campaign finance laws, which control who can con-

 ## WHERE AMERICANS LIVE: ETHNIC DISTRIBUTION

Geographic distribution of America's population tends to fall along ethnic lines. The 1990 U.S. census reported that Americans of the most common European ancestry were evenly distributed across the nation while other European-origin groups were concentrated in various regions: Italian Americans in the Northeast; Czechoslovakian and Norwegian Americans in the Midwest; just under half of the Scottish and Irish Americans in the South; and just under half of the Danish Americans in the West. Hispanic Americans are dispersed largely according to country of origin: Most Dominicans and Ecuadorians are concentrated in the Northeast; most Cubans and Nicaraguans in the South; and most Salvadorans, Guatemalans, and Mexicans in the West.

Most Asian Americans and those of Pacific Island origins live in the West, including large majorities of people from Hawaii, Japan, Cambodia, China, and Vietnam. America's most populous state, California, contains the most citizens of German, Irish, English, African American, Mexican, French, Native American, Dutch, Scotch-Irish, Scottish, and Swedish ancestry of any state; New York has more Italians and Poles than any other state.

tribute money to candidates and put restrictions on the amounts, are in need of reform. But members of Congress do not agree on exactly how these reforms should be accomplished, so the relevant bills have languished several years without major debate or the opportunity for a final vote.

THE EXECUTIVE BRANCH: THE U.S. PRESIDENT

Congress passes the nation's federal laws, but it is up to another branch, the executive, to see that these laws are carried out. The executive branch is led by the president of the United States, who serves as both the chief of state (speaking and acting for the whole nation on ceremonial occasions) and as the head of government, making decisions that directly affect the lives of everyone in the country. Through the appointed heads of agencies like the Department of State, the Department of the Treasury, and the Department of Justice, the president sees to it that America's wishes are known abroad, that the nation's money is respected as a means of buying goods and services, and that the nation's laws are enforced. As one of only two public servants elected on a nationwide basis (the vice president is the other), the president also sets the nation's legislative priorities each year. These are expressed through the State of the Union address and the proposed federal budget.

One of the most important roles assigned to U.S. presidents under the Constitution is that of commander in chief of America's armed forces. Although the Constitution assigns Congress the sole power to declare war, throughout American history many presidents have introduced U.S. forces into combat without seeking a formal declaration from Congress. For example, in the last fifty years presidents have sent troops to places like Korea, Vietnam, and Serbia without formal declarations of war. However, presidents know that they cannot commit U.S. troops to a sustained conflict without broad public support for such policies and without funding from Congress. Accordingly, U.S. presidents often find that their real power lies less in dictating policy than in leadership and persuasion. President Harry Truman (1945–1952) humorously observed, "All a president is, is a glorified public relations man who spends his time flattering, kissing, and kicking people to get them to do what they are supposed to do anyway."[33]

THE JUDICIAL BRANCH: U.S. FEDERAL COURTS

The legislative branch makes the laws and the executive carries them out, but it is the third branch that determines whether those laws and actions are constitutional. The judicial branch is led by the U.S. Supreme Court, which oversees a broad system of federal district courts. The justices who serve in the judicial branch are appointed by the president, but these appointments must be approved by Congress. Federal judges are appointed for life, which means they need not leave office except voluntarily or in cases of severe misconduct. Since federal justices cannot be fired for political reasons, they are free to exercise their best judgment without fear of political backlash.

U.S. federal courts have the power to rule for plaintiffs or defendants in lawsuits that arise among U.S. citizens, or between citizens and the federal government, so long as these cases are governed by state or federal statutes. The Supreme Court also has the final authority to interpret the Constitu-

The Supreme Court building houses the highest court in the United States. The Supreme Court has the power to interpret the Constitution and nullify laws passed by Congress.

tion; thus, it can nullify any law passed by Congress if it finds that law to be contrary to the Constitution. In the past two hundred years or so, the Court has struck down over 1,000 state laws and some 125 federal laws, in whole or in part. For example, when Congress passed a law giving the president authority to exercise a line-item veto—that is, to veto individual sections of bills passed by Congress rather than signing or vetoing entire bills—a majority of the Supreme Court's justices said such authority gave the president improper power to modify laws passed by Congress.

Supreme Court justices function as legal servants whose jobs are supposed to be far removed from the shifting tides of public opinion. Supreme Court justices are often controversial for their rulings, and of all of the top U.S. government officials, they are the least known to their fellow citizens. Still, they are generally among America's best-respected government leaders for their intellectual and political integrity.

STATE AND LOCAL GOVERNMENTS

For all of its power to directly affect Americans' daily lives, the federal government is only part of the story of how free people govern themselves. The United States includes fifty separate states and many dependent areas, ranging from American Samoa and Guam in the Pacific to Puerto Rico and the Virgin Islands in the Caribbean. America's fifty state governments are organized much like its federal government, with a state constitution establishing a chief executive or governor; state legislatures that create state laws, impose state taxes, and spend state revenues; and a state supreme court that is the highest authority in interpreting state law (although state supreme court decisions can be appealed to the U.S. Supreme Court).

These fifty states play the leading role in creating and administering public education, transportation, and safety along with certain environmental regulations and consumer protection. No state is allowed to create its own currency or postal service, and states may not pass laws that conflict with federal laws or with the U.S. Constitution. Within each state, a system of county and city governments provides basic services, including power, water, police, and fire fighting. State and county governments are typically run by mayors, city councils, school boards, and county judges, many of whom are elected officials. It is through this vast network of public officials that the American people's business is done. How these officials interpret and carry out the needs and will of an increasingly diverse population is the real story of America's government.

THE POLITICS OF RACE

American society includes members of virtually every race, ethnic group, religion, national origin, and language of the world. Accordingly, U.S. political leaders make many of their policy decisions with America's racial, ethnic, linguistic, generational, and religious diversity firmly in mind, attempting to obey the majority's will while also promoting the agenda, rights, and interests of minorities. Approximately 80 percent of Americans are white, 12 percent are black; 3 percent are Asian or Pacific Islander, and 1 percent are Native American, Eskimo, or Aleut; almost 4 percent identify themselves by other racial labels. Among these racial or ethnic groups, 9 percent of Americans identify themselves as Hispanic in origin.

U.S. citizens are a diverse mix of different races, ethnicities, and cultural backgrounds, contributing to the idea of the United States as a melting pot.

MELTING POT OR SALAD BOWL?

America's unique mixture of races and heritages produces a complex sense of personal identity for many U.S. citizens. The national ideal has long been a melting pot in which all citizens become something called an American. The reality, however, sometimes resembles a salad bowl, consisting of elements that exist side by side in a vigorous mixture yet retain their unique qualities nonetheless.

President Teddy Roosevelt once complained about what he called hyphenated Americanism: citizens who label themselves "Irish-Americans," "German-Americans," and so on. In a powerful poem for a school program called "I, Too, Am America," a Los Angeles eighth-grader expressed the quandry that many ethnic Americans feel. Her poem was later published in the February 5, 1999, edition of the *Los Angeles Times:*

> How can you label me?
> My mother's from Guatemala,
> My father's from Honduras,
> My grandmother's from Belize,
> My grandfather's from Jamaica.
> And it goes back so much further.
> I speak English and Spanish.
> So do you label me Hispanic?
> Or Black-Hispanic?
> Or "Blaxican"?
> Here's an idea:
> Don't label me at all.

Many important U.S. government policy debates revolve around apportioning power, opportunity, and public funds among the country's various racial and ethnic groups. For example, to overcome past discrimination, successive U.S. presidential administrations and congresses have embraced a philosophy called affirmative action. Laws, regulations, and government policies reflecting this philosophy encourage the hiring of qualified minorities in the workplace. Affirmative action policies also set aside grants and a certain percentage of government contracts for minority-owned businesses. In addition to encouraging diversity in the workplace through affirmative action, the federal government may also require sometimes-complex formulas to achieve racial and ethnic balance in public schools.

Most Americans support the ideal of integrated schools, but there have been stormy protests, and even lawsuits, when one group perceives its rights as having been sacrificed in the interests of less-qualified members of other groups. For example, when the locally elected school board tried to adjust the ethnic balance of a school for the academically gifted in San Francisco by screening out better-qualified students of Vietnamese origin in favor of less-qualified Chinese American students, Vietnamese American parents complained. Ultimately, it is the job of government—either elected officials or judges—to find a way to balance competing claims of this sort.

THE POLITICS OF AGE AND GENDER

The median age in America is 35, but U.S. census figures show a broad range of age groups. Like race and ethnicity, this demographic factor also leads to conflicts that the government is required to resolve. Ongoing age-related political issues involve how much money should be taken out of workers' paychecks to finance Social Security as well as whether a rapidly growing population of elders can be financially supported in the future by the Social Security contributions of a smaller group of wage earners. How to regulate and pay for the skyrocketing costs of health care, particularly for older Americans, generates additional political and economic debates. Additional age-related political issues include disagreements over the rights and qualifications of very young (and very old) drivers and the minimum drinking age (U.S. citizens can vote and be drafted into the armed forces at age eighteen, but they cannot drink until age twenty-one).

Among those old enough to work full time—and too young to qualify for a Social Security pension—America's population is split about equally between men and women. Gender issues in U.S. politics include securing equal pay and equal opportunity for women. Just as it is true in the politics of race, legislatures have passed laws to protect both men and women from gender discrimination. Courts are often called on to force employers, schools, and other public facilities to offer equal opportunities to women and men.

THE POLITICS OF LANGUAGE AND RELIGION

America's diversity of language provides additional occasions for political debate and action. Most Americans speak English, although there is a large minority of Spanish speakers. Virtually every other known language and dialect on the earth can be found somewhere in the United States. Americans frequently disagree over language-related issues, and these debates often break down along racial and ethnic lines. For example, over twenty U.S. states have passed laws making English their official language and requiring all public signs to be posted in English only. Speakers of other languages—most prominently Spanish—often resist this idea, believing that it ignores not only their native tongue but also their culture, ethnicity, and heritage. There have even been proposals to adopt English as the entire nation's official language. Whether an amendment is passed enshrining English in the U.S. Constitution will be determined by Congress and individual state legislatures, voting in accordance with the will of the voters.

Religion provides even more occasions for political controversies. Americans as a whole report themselves as quite religious: A large majority say they believe in God, life after death, and the existence of good and evil. A growing number say they believe in angels and Satan, too. Most Americans practice Christianity: 61 percent of all U.S. citizens are Protestant; 25 percent are Catholic. About 10 percent of Americans profess no religion. The country's 2 percent Jewish population (about 5.4 million people) makes up the world's largest concentration of Jews outside of Israel. Sizable numbers of Americans practice Islam, Buddhism, and Hinduism, to name just a few others. This vigorous religious mix leads to healthy debate and disagreement over the proper role of religion in U.S. public life. The U.S. Constitution guarantees freedom of religion and prohibits the establishment of any official religion. The Supreme Court has interpreted the clause as requiring strict separation of church and state. Americans continue to debate, sue, and pass laws regarding separation, including whether religious symbols may be displayed in public spaces or public schools may set aside special time for prayer or post the Ten Commandments in classrooms. It is the people's will, as expressed through their elected representatives, that decides

In a scene from the Bible depicting the resurrection of Jesus, an angel beckons mourners to the now-empty site where Jesus' body had lain. Biblical stories such as this are part of America's Christian heritage.

many of these questions; other issues are resolved by courts, where the intent of America's founders, as expressed in the Constitution, is determined.

THE POLITICS OF EDUCATION

Americans strongly value education, so government representatives at all levels constantly seek improved education policies. Some Americans prize a high degree of local control of their public schools: In their view, all decisions regarding schools should be made by locally elected officials. Others advocate establishing national academic standards, curricula, and testing, which would greatly reduce local control of schools. This debate is played out at many levels, ranging from local school boards to Congress and even to the U.S. Supreme Court. Congress grants federal money that states can use on educational programs, but whether a state gets the money depends on its compliance with various federal education policies. For example, colleges that comply with federal laws mandating equal opportunities and facilities for men and women in athletics receive full federal funding; colleges that fail to achieve such gender equity may risk losing millions of dollars.

The federal government is only one source of money for schools. At the elementary and secondary levels, money collected in the form of local taxes supports most educational activities. And how to make certain that school-age children all get a quality education, regardless of the wealth of the local community, is a subject of constant debate among Americans. Through their elected state officials and by voting on various proposals for funding their local schools, Americans determine how much money will be available to pay teachers, buy books, and even build new school buildings.

THE ROLE OF POLITICAL PARTIES

Alexis de Tocqueville, perhaps the most gifted interpreter of the American character, long ago observed in his classic work *Democracy in America* that U.S. citizens have a passion for organizing themselves into voluntary civic groups. The most visible and influential of America's voluntary associations are its major political parties. (Although the U.S. Constitution makes no explicit provision for political parties, it does not forbid them either.) The two leading U.S. political parties are the Democrats and the Republicans. Their respective organizations—along with, to a far lesser extent, dozens of smaller parties—play a vital role in America's political process. From the local to the state and national levels, political parties nominate candidates for public office, including county commissioners, state senators and representatives, governors, federal representatives and senators, and presidents and vice presidents. Once they nominate candidates for public offices, political parties dole out money that is used for political advertisements on radio and television and for other campaign activities like travel by the candidates and the staging of public rallies. In fact, the ability of the two leading political parties to raise and distribute large amounts of money has itself become the subject of debate in America.

BILL CLINTON, FORTY-SECOND PRESIDENT OF THE UNITED STATES

Born in Arkansas in 1946, William Jefferson Clinton was a good student whose passion for politics started early. At age seventeen, as a participant in the American Legion's Boy's Nation program, he met President John F. Kennedy at the White House and at that time decided to enter public service himself someday. Educated at George Washington University, Oxford, and Yale Law School, Clinton worked in the 1972 Democratic presidential campaign and ran successfully for Arkansas attorney general in 1976. Clinton served five terms as the state's governor, working to improve public education while encouraging business investments that created more jobs in the state.

Clinton was elected president in 1992 at age forty-six, becoming the third-youngest American ever to achieve that office. He was reelected in 1996. Both as a candidate and as president, Clinton has criticized traditional political ideologies and promoted a "middle way" or creative synthesis between liberal and conservative ideas. Clinton's economic policies are widely credited with helping to encourage and sustain the longest peacetime economic boom in U.S. history, but his political course has been rocky at times. In late 1998 he became the second president in U.S. history to undergo impeachment in the House of Representatives (the charges of perjury and obstruction of justice stemmed from a sexual harassment case). But in early 1999 he won his Senate trial and enjoyed the highest popularity ratings of his presidency.

Minor political parties rarely elect leaders to public office, but they do play a useful role in the American political process. Often a small political party serves to raise issues that have been largely ignored by the two leading parties. A minor party may educate the public about such issues and help create a demand for action. For example, in the 1990s the Reform Party provided a vehicle for millions of Americans to express their discontent with campaign finance laws that allow wealthy individuals and organizations to contribute millions of dollars, directly or indirectly, to political candidates. Many Americans of all political stripes agree that such contributions can result in contributors' receiving disproportionate influence on the legislative process. Other citizens firmly believe that the Constitution's guarantee of free speech protects, or should protect, unrestricted campaign contributions. Both major parties have called for change, but little has actually been done in recent years to amend the current system. Partially as a result of this situation, Reform Party candidate Ross Perot received tens of millions of votes in the 1992 presidential election. At the time, many observers questioned whether Perot's strong presence in the race may have indirectly assisted the ultimate winner, Democratic candidate Bill Clinton, to achieve his election victory with less than 50 percent of the popular vote.

DYNAMIC INTERPLAY BETWEEN
THE PEOPLE AND THE GOVERNMENT

On the whole, then, U.S. national life involves a complex, dynamic interplay between the American people and their government. In the Declaration of Independence, Thomas Jefferson originally spoke of the American experience in terms of "life, liberty, and the pursuit of happiness." Today, Americans cheerfully pursue their life goals in a structure of "liberty within law"—a structure designed to provide the greatest possible happiness for the greatest possible number of U.S. citizens and inhabitants. According to President Clinton,

> If we continue to follow the opportunity-responsibility-community strategy which has brought us so far, we will build an America that is leading the world to greater peace and freedom and prosperity, an America coming together on the strength of our marvelous diversity, an America where all of our children, wherever they start in life, will have a chance to live their dreams.[34]

6

"I HEAR AMERICA SINGING": MANY VOICES, MANY CULTURES

Even before the founding of the United States, Americans had begun the process of creating an entirely new culture. Their collective voice grew from a mixture that was partly European and partly Native American; later, America's cultural blend also reflected growing African and Asian influences. The result of this vigorous mix has been a sprawling 250-year eruption of new art forms and new cultural ideals in the high arts, folk arts, and popular culture. Drawing from wide-ranging influences, American art forms celebrate the rebellious loner character who is the frequent hero of U.S. fiction, the lively rhythms of jazz and tap dancing, the no-limits architecture of city skyscrapers, homegrown American sports such as baseball and the rodeo, folk arts such as quilting and barbed-wire decoration, and popular arts and mass media such as motion pictures and commercial broadcasting. Americans have also actively pursued fine arts such as painting and sculpture. All of these new forms and ideals tend to demonstrate the self-confidence and self-assertiveness that the world instantly perceives as uniquely American.

Extreme critics have charged that the phrase American culture is a contradiction in terms. They maintain that Americans are too obsessed with money to cultivate true art, and whatever art America has is loud, ugly, violent, trashy, and shallow. The American journalist H. L. Mencken may have partially confirmed this critique when he observed that "Nobody ever went broke underestimating the American public."[35] But America contains many publics, and these in turn ardently support many cultures and many artistic visions. Perhaps those who find nothing to applaud on the U.S. arts scene simply have not been looking hard enough. Poet Walt Whitman beautifully expressed the awakening nation's diversity of creative stirrings: "I hear America singing; the varied carols I hear."[36]

MODERN AMERICAN LITERATURE: MANY QUESTIONS, FEW ANSWERS

In many ways, the chief subject of American writers has always been America itself: its land, its people, the meaning of the American experiment, and that experiment's ultimate chances for success. "American writers are constantly writing about American identity, as if it were something that was yet to be discovered,"[37] commented Canadian critic Paul Levine. Defining the American character and illuminating the American experience "is the great chore, task or challenge our writers have always dealt with," agreed Pulitzer Prize–winning novelist E. L. Doctorow. He confirmed that America's identity always does "remain to be discovered" since "this is a very young country, and it is a polyglot mixture that is still forming itself through waves of immigration."[38]

Baseball, a uniquely American sport, is a favorite pastime of many Americans to both watch and play.

Since the end of World War II, American writers have expressed what critic Leslie Fiedler calls the end of innocence—the loss of faith in earlier certainties and traditional values like patriotism, religion, marriage, community, and even the stability and predictability of the physical world. Novelists like Toni Morrison, E. L. Doctorow, Richard Wright, Thomas Pynchon, and Norman Mailer, along with poets like Allen Ginsberg, have depicted the tragic costs of political corruption and the savage ironies of social injustice.

For example, the novel *Beloved,* which won Morrison the 1993 Nobel Prize for literature, focuses on Sethe, a former slave who is haunted by the ghost of a daughter she chose to murder rather than risk permitting that child to grow up in slavery. The novel questions which act is truly the greater evil—killing the body through murder or killing the soul through slavery. It also suggests that America, like Sethe herself, remains tragically haunted by the aftermath of slavery. In a similar vein, Doctorow's *The Book of Daniel* questions the meaning, and indeed the very reality, of American freedom. This story focuses on the children of two parents who were wrongly executed for espionage during the height of America's anti-Communist hysteria. Doctorow implies that much of what Americans take to be freedom is an illusion, and he suggests that wealth—not individual liberty—might be the nation's highest value.

Yet amidst such sharp questioning and criticism, some of America's most important twentieth-century writers have remained convinced of the virtues traditionally prized by Americans: individual bravery, directness, simplicity, being close to nature, and independence. Ernest Hemingway, for example, celebrated the physical and moral courage of his protagonist Santiago in his novella *The Old Man and the Sea.* The tough old fisherman exhibits what Hemingway called grace under pressure: He lands a huge marlin all by himself, then battles sharks that eat away at his catch. When these predators at last deprive Santiago of his fish, he remains stoic. One of the most accomplished stylists in modern prose, Hemingway's spare yet poetically suggestive use of language remains widely influential among contemporary American writers, even those—like Morrison—who hold deeply divergent philosophies or worldviews.

America's Music Scene

America's wide blend of cultural influences also gave birth to vibrant new forms of music and dance. Measured in terms of sales, rock and its offshoot, rap (also called hip-hop), are the most popular American musical forms. Rock originated as dance music in the United States in the 1950s, offering a simple yet powerful beat and driving rhythms with drums and guitars to express the exuberance (and sometimes the frustration) of youth. Rock-style dancing broke with all previous rules, abandoning prescribed forms and requiring only that dancers move rhythmically to the beat. Popularized by radio and records alike, rock grew into one of the world's most popular types of music, drawing influences from all over the globe that infused the music with fresh sounds and growing audiences.

In contrast to the ever-revolutionary world of rock, many Americans enjoy more traditional music called country or country and western. This music usually tells a story with simple, clear lyrics, and it often focuses on love and romance but sometimes deals with patriotic themes. Songs are delivered in a clear, easily understandable voice, supported chiefly by string instruments. Springing from folk music of the 1800s, country music had achieved its all-time peak of popularity by the mid-1990s with artists like Garth Brooks, whose hits included songs like "The Thunder Rolls" and "We Shall Be Free."

Jazz

Many observers of the arts regard another form of music, jazz, as America's only completely original art form. The music that later evolved into jazz was created and played by black Americans in New Orleans in the early 1800s. Jazz came from a mixture of African rhythms, European harmonies, and American band instruments (such as the banjo). Jazz continues to develop its sound, but it always features improvisation, strong rhythm sections, and unusual phrasing and rhythmic accents (called syncopation). Through these elements, jazz conveys a spirit so lively and spontaneous that it has been nicknamed "the Music of Freedom."

Jazz was one of America's most popular musical forms from the 1920s through the 1940s, but it took a back seat to rock from the 1950s through the 1980s. However, jazz continues to exert a strong influence on other types of American

Louis Armstrong, one of the most prominent musicians of the twentieth century, helped popularize jazz, a form of music that originated in the United States.

music—it even influenced some U.S. classical music, as heard in the joyful rhythms of George Gershwin's 1924 symphonic composition "Rhapsody in Blue." Beginning in the 1990s, jazz enjoyed a major resurgence. Today, live bands and orchestras increasingly play Duke Ellington's compositions from the 1930s to the 1950s, and his original recordings are more popular than ever in CD releases.

CLASSICAL

Classical music attracts a relatively small but fiercely dedicated audience in the United States. The presence of a symphony orchestra led by a recognized conductor is a sign that an American city has "arrived" culturally. The nation's major orchestras (as measured by sales of their recordings) reside in New York, Boston, Philadelphia, Chicago, and St. Louis. Additional successful orchestras can also be found in San Francisco; Los Angeles; Dallas; Denver; Washington, D.C.; and other smaller American cities. Opera performances, once viewed as an upper-class indulgence, enjoyed their greatest level of popularity in America during the 1990s, selling out virtually every performance by major opera companies around the country. But when visitors to the United States arrive at most ports of entry, they are greeted by a very different art form: Amercian architecture.

Reaching for New Heights: American Architecture

In 1884 a new type of building began to rise in Chicago's business district: a ten-story structure with a metal frame. It was the Home Insurance Company Building, designed by architect William Le Baron Jenney. Over the next century, as new materials and technologies such as steel beams, elevators, and air conditioning appeared, American architects reached toward the clouds with ever taller spires of glass and steel. Led by Chicago's Louis Henry Sullivan, these designers expressed their visions of humankind's limitless possibilities in buildings whose dizzying heights were previously thought impossible. New York and Chicago especially became famous for these daring new structures, which were dubbed skyscrapers.

The skyscraper is an expression of Americans' love of testing limits and their tendency to find practical solutions to problems. Where open land is limited or expensive, skyscrapers allow builders to provide vertical space. Built upon deep underground foundations, a skyscraper can rise far over one thousand feet in the air—so high that wind forces against its sides become a greater engineering factor than the structure's overall weight. Some skyscraper complexes

Jazz Meets Classical: The Odyssey of Wynton Marsalis

The first jazz composer to win a prestigious Pulitzer Prize for music was Wynton Marsalis. This gifted trumpeter excels as both a jazz and classical musician. Born in 1961 in the same city as jazz itself—New Orleans—Marsalis combines musical passion and openness to innovation, with exacting technique. He loves both the history and the feeling—the soul—of jazz. His educational zeal for this American music form, along with his disciplined talent, has made him one of the music world's most influential and popular artists.

Young Marsalis learned both his craft and his art from a series of teachers that included his father, respected jazz pianist Ellis Marsalis. He was performing classical trumpet concertos with the New Orleans Symphony by age fourteen. Marsalis recorded his first albums in 1980 with Art Blakey's band, later leading his own groups and recording under his own name in both the classical and jazz fields. Since 1991 Marsalis has served as artistic director of New York City's "Jazz at Lincoln Center" program.

include clusters of related buildings; they offer so much space and house so many functions that they become virtually self-contained cities with business offices, hotels, restaurants, apartments, condominiums, retail stores, health clubs, and even warehouses.

Skyscrapers make artistic statements about the practical beauty of steel-and-glass engineering. America's modern architects often express their aesthetic in the catchphrase *form follows function*. The race to build ever taller skyscrapers is tapering off as new metropolitan growth patterns and new communications technologies make it less urgent to concentrate businesses and people in compact downtown areas. But commanding skylines still characterize many large U.S. cities, and America's skyscrapers remain impressive monuments to an era of national self-confidence and innovation.

Within and around America's cities, the nation's artists add their distinctive touches to art forms like painting and sculpture. During the last few decades of the twentieth century, both forms largely moved away from depicting people,

The Empire State Building towers over its neighbors in New York, a city famous for its enormous skyscrapers.

FRANK LLOYD WRIGHT'S "ORGANIC" ARCHITECTURE

America's most important architect is generally acknowledged to be Frank Lloyd Wright. This midwestern maverick believed a home should reflect its owners' personalities and enhance their daily lives. Wright designed bold, modern private residences and artfully integrated these structures into their natural surroundings. Wright accomplished this by subtly echoing natural shapes and forms in his overall plans and by employing raw materials found in the region for construction. Often, large windows created a feeling of continuity between a home's interior spaces and its outside environment. Wright's 1936 masterpiece, Fallingwater, sits directly over a rural Pennsylvania stream and waterfall.

Later in his career, Wright designed churches, offices, and other public buildings. Playful structures like his spiral-ramped Guggenheim Museum in New York have influenced architects around the world. Original Wright designs continue to be built—his Madison, Wisconsin, city hall was recently erected after a fifty-year delay—and graduates of two architecture schools founded by Wright carry on his principles and traditions.

---

objects, and scenes as they would be seen by the human eye. Traditional landscapes and human figures have often given way to abstract shapes. Even the media that some American artists are using for their work have changed. For example, in the 1990s American painters such as Julian Schnabel have explored the limits of painting by adding three-dimensional items, including broken bits of crockery, to the paint and canvas. Such experimental art forms suggest an unrestrained intellectual playfulness, but it is sheer physical playfulness that the greatest number of Americans enjoy—particularly in the form of organized sports and outdoor leisure activities.

AMERICAN SPORTS AND LEISURE

Americans have been described, paradoxically, both as workaholics and as sports fanatics. Both descriptions are true. According to a September 1999 report by the International Labor Organization, Americans work "longer hours than anyone else in the industrialized world"[39]—an average of 1,966 hours per year, or (assuming two weeks' vacation,

GLENNA GOODACRE, AMERICAN SCULPTOR

A new U.S. dollar coin entered circulation early in the year 2000. Its obverse design features a beautiful portrait of Sacagawea, the Native American woman of the Shoshone tribe who guided U.S. explorers Lewis and Clark to the Pacific Ocean in the early 1800s. Sacagawea is seen carrying her infant son on her back, just as the historical seventeen-year-old guide really did throughout her arduous journey.

This striking image was created by Glenna Goodacre, one of America's most accomplished modern sculptors. A graduate of Colorado College, Goodacre is best known for the bronze Vietnam Women's Memorial in Washington, D.C.

Goodacre is one of the few contemporary sculptors to win both critical and popular acclaim by creating realistic yet idealized human forms. For much of this century, serious sculpture has celebrated abstract, unrecognizable shapes or has imaginatively envisioned the human body. Not only has Goodacre's work received widespread popular appreciation, she has also won many awards from the National Sculpture Society and the National Academy of Design. With billions of units of the new coin in circulation, people around the world now have a chance to enjoy her work firsthand.

plus holidays) just over 40 hours per week. The number of hours that Americans work has been slowly but steadily rising since 1980, the same study reports. However, this fact may only prompt Americans to play with even greater zeal and intensity when they are away from their jobs.

Each week millions of Americans watch professional sports teams in homegrown sports like football, baseball, basketball, and hockey, and millions more participate in an enormous range of recreational activities, including visiting zoos, picnicking, pleasure driving, jogging, walking, playing amateur sports, camping, fishing, hiking, and attending cultural events. One measure of the importance of sports and leisure in American life is the amount of money invested in such activities: Americans spend over $200 billion a year on leisure in all of its varied aspects.

Of America's best-known sports, baseball is so popular that it is often considered to be the national pastime. This one sport attracts 50 million visitors to stadiums each spring and summer, and millions more watch baseball games on television. In addition, amateur baseball is played by organized teams for every age group, ranging from six-year-olds to senior citizens. Many baseball fans take the game so seriously that they can recite obscure sports statistics from decades past, and many amateur baseball players take the sport so seriously that even senior league tournaments now post hundreds of thousands of dollars in prizes.

Turning Technology into New Art Forms

U.S. citizens often speak with pride of Yankee ingenuity: They like to think of themselves as practical, down-to-earth people who love new gadgets and technological innovation. But America's ongoing fascination with new technologies is frequently channeled into aesthetic and communications purposes, generating exciting new art forms and powerful new media. Film is one obvious example. Beginning in 1893, when American inventor Thomas Edison unveiled the world's first commercial movie machine, and continuing a century later as American firms revolutionize special effects, sound, and theatrical presentation through digital technology, American innovations have continually extended the capabilities and scope of this vast and powerful medium.

Americans sometimes question the impact of certain movies, especially on younger viewers. Americans perpetually debate whether and how much the movies' depiction of crime leads viewers to emulate what they see onscreen. But for good or ill, American movies win millions of viewers daily. They help dramatize and personify the nation's self-image, both to its own citizens and (as one of the nation's leading cultural exports) to the rest of the world. In the eyes of some, a film such as *Forrest Gump* portrays what is best about America and Americans. According to director-screenwriter Robert Zemeckis, "For me, Forrest Gump is in fact a metaphor for the American character in the last half of the twentieth century"[40]—bumbling but well intentioned, powerful but innocent to the point of naïveté.

Electronic Media in America

If Americans are fascinated by images on the big screen of a movie theater, they are obsessed with images on the small

The Internet provides Americans and the world at large with a powerful tool for communication, research, and entertainment.

screens of their televisions. On average, Americans spend six hours per day watching TV. Of this time, perhaps an hour or less falls under the strict heading of news, but that percentage is growing as topically oriented talk shows, televised "newsmagazines," and so-called infotainment programming steadily grow in quantity and popularity. As free people, Americans have a natural need and desire to know the latest developments in politics, business, science, art, and even sports. American news media—both in print and electronic formats—tirelessly feed this appetite with a never-ending flow of reporting, information, exposés, opinion, and, increasingly, gossip and unconfirmed rumor. But an even more wide-open medium beckons not just Americans but also people the world over.

The latest technology to explode into a brand-new communications free-for-all is the Internet. The Internet and its graphically oriented subset, the World Wide Web, act as the central nervous system for most of the planet's on-line computers and databases. At little or no cost, a single individual or group can post images, text, or data on the Internet for instant worldwide dispersal. In 1969 U.S. scientists working for the federal government constructed the "Net" as a network of networks. Its purpose was to allow various defense industry computers to "talk" to each other over telephone lines. By the 1990s the Internet had evolved into a runaway technology for the general public around the world.

The Internet is so new that its full implications have yet to be recognized. But in a few short years, it has already revolutionized personal and business communications, the news media, and commerce. Private individuals, small businesses, large corporations, and governments constantly use the Net to e-mail text and images back and forth. Many of these Net users have also created websites that can be accessed via the Internet and displayed simultaneously on millions of desktop computers around the world. Websites can function as electronic billboards, newspapers, magazines, radio and television stations, retail stores, instant auction markets, or a combination of these.

New Expressions of America's Original Creed

Over four hundred years ago America began as a new frontier for courageous European explorers. It blossomed into a nation that was an experiment in liberty, creating a new frontier for political, religious, and individual freedoms. This experimental nation developed into a physical frontier for pioneers, cowboys, farmers, and homesteaders; these pioneers eventually conquered much of the North American continent. During the twentieth century, America's restless people expanded their commercial and military reach over half of the globe, visited the Moon, and finally united much of the planet in cyberspace.

Today, the restless people called Americans race to create brand-new technological and psychological frontiers for their unique, wide-open styles of art and communication. Through these new media, Americans will continue to pursue and promote new frontiers of innovation in business, science, and commerce. Americans will also continue to cultivate the many voices and multiple cultures that make the United States a unique nation of nations.

During the twenty-first century, the United States will no doubt continue its expansion, elaboration, and re-creation of its revolutionary American experiment in liberty.

FACTS ABOUT THE UNITED STATES

GOVERNMENT

Founded: 1776

Type of government: constitutional democratic republic; federal system of national, state, and local authority

Number of states: 50

National capital: Washington, D.C.

LAND

Land area: 3,536,341 square miles

Share of global acreage: 6.2%

Northernmost point: Point Barrow, Alaska

Easternmost point: West Quoddy Head, Maine

Southernmost point: Ka Lae, Hawaii

Westernmost point: Cape Wrangell, Alaska

Geographic center (including Alaska and Hawaii): Butte County, South Dakota

Geographic center (48 coterminous states): near Lebanon, Kansas

Largest city: New York (population 7 million)

Climate: mostly temperate

PEOPLE

Population: 270 million

Annual population growth: 0.87%

Birthrate: 14.5 births per 1,000 people (1997 estimate)

Death rate: 8.6 deaths per 1,000 people (1997 estimate)

Life expectancy: 76 years

Median age: 35 years

Number of families: 70 million (1997 estimate)

Average household size: 3.19 (1997 estimate)

Languages: mainly English, with a large Spanish-speaking minority

Literacy rate: 97%

Racial/Ethnic Composition: 80% white, 12% black, 3% Asian, 0.8% Native American, 4% other. Ethnically, 9% of people in the preceding racial categories identify themselves as Hispanic.

Religion: 60% identify themselves with an organized religion; of these 52% are Protestant; 38% Roman Catholic; 4% Jewish; 3% Mormon; 3% Eastern Orthodox. Less than 1% belong to other faiths such as Islam or Buddhism.

Education: 78% earn high-school diplomas; 24% obtain college degrees

ECONOMY

Monetary unit: dollar

Economic structure: mixed economy (regulated capitalism)

Gross domestic product: $8 trillion/year

Federal budget: $1.6 trillion (1998 estimate)

Exports: $625 billion (1996 estimate)

Imports: $822 billion (1996 estimate)

Major trading partners: Canada, Japan, Western Europe

Chief crops: corn, wheat, barley, oats, sugar, potatoes, soybeans, fruits, beef, veal, pork

Natural resources: coal, oil, copper, gold, silver, minerals, timber

Key industries: petroleum products, fertilizers, cement, iron and steel, plastics and resins, newsprint, motor vehicles, machinery, natural gas, aerospace, electronics, computers, communications

Workforce: 136 million workers

Unemployment rate: 4.3% (1999 estimate)

Average per-capita income: $28,500/year

Median family income: $51,518 (1996 estimate)

Home ownership: 64% of population

Poverty rate: 13% of population

NOTES

CHAPTER 1: THE AMERICAN EXPERIMENT: "A REPUBLIC— IF YOU CAN KEEP IT"

1. Interview with the author in Los Angeles, California, July 17, 1999.

2. Quoted in interview with the author.

3. Quoted in Paul M. Angle, ed., *By These Words—Great Documents of American Liberty.* New York: Rand McNally, 1968, p. 93.

4. Quoted in Richard L. Park, ed., *The American Revolution Abroad.* Philadelphia: American Academy of Political and Social Science, 1976, p. 22.

5. Quoted in Barbara W. Tuchman, *The First Salute.* New York: Knopf, 1988, p. 187.

6. Henry Steele Commager and Richard B. Morris, eds., *The Spirit of 'Seventy-Six: The Story of the American Revolution As Told by Participants.* New York: Harper & Row, 1976, p. xxxiv.

7. Quoted in Park, *The American Revolution Abroad,* p. 23.

8. Quoted in *American Historical Review,* vol. 11, 1906, p. 618.

9. Quoted in Maureen Harrison and Steve Gilbert, eds., *George Washington in His Own Words.* New York: Barnes & Noble Books, 1997, p. 184.

CHAPTER 2: "LET FREEDOM RING": EXPANDING THE FRONTIERS OF LIBERTY

10. Quoted in Carl Sandburg, *Abraham Lincoln—the Prairie Years and the War Years.* New York: Harcourt Brace Jovanovich, 1942, p. 138.

11. Quoted in Brian MacArthur, ed., *The Penguin Book of Twentieth-Century Speeches.* New York: Penguin Books, 1992, p. 55.

12. Ronald Reagan, inscription in *Tampico High School Yearbook,* 1928, on display at the Ronald Reagan Presidential Li-

brary, Simi Valley, California.

13. Quoted in MacArthur, *The Penguin Book of Twentieth-Century Speeches,* p. 124.

14. Quoted in Russell Freedman, *Franklin Delano Roosevelt.* New York: Clarion Books/Houghton Mifflin, 1990, p. 1.

15. Quoted in MacArthur, *The Penguin Book of Twentieth-Century Speeches,* p. 194.

16. Quoted in MacArthur, *The Penguin Book of Twentieth-Century Speeches,* p. 334.

17. Gerald R. Ford, "Remarks on Assuming the Presidency of the United States," August 9, 1974. Gerald R. Ford Library and Museum, www.ford.utexas/edu/library/speeches/740001.htm.

CHAPTER 3: AN ECONOMIC SUPERPOWER: THE CREATIVE ENERGIES OF FREE PEOPLE

18. Thomas L. Friedman, "An American in Paris," *New York Times,* August 20, 1999, p. A-12.

19. Robert L. McCan and William H. Peterson, "An Outline of the American Economy," U.S. Information Agency, 1991. www.usia.gov/usa/infousa/trade/ameconom/.

20. Quoted in Joel Kotkin, "The New Ethnic Entrepreneurs," *Los Angeles Times,* September 12, 1999, p. M-2.

21. Quoted in Ford R. Bryan, *Beyond the Model T: The Other Ventures of Henry Ford.* Detroit: Wayne State University Press, 1990, p. 54.

22. Bill Clinton, *Between Hope and History: Meeting America's Challenges for the Twenty-First Century.* New York: Times Books/Random House, 1996, p. 95.

23. Quoted in MacArthur, *The Penguin Book of Twentieth-Century Speeches,* p. 441.

24. Barry Goldwater, "Address to the Veterans of Foreign Wars," Sheraton Park Hotel, Washington, DC, March 25, 1975.

25. Don Lee and Nancy Cleeland, "State's Boom Brings More Job Insecurity, Study Says," *Los Angeles Times,* May 25, 1999, p. C-1.

26. Clinton, *Between Hope and History,* p. 50.

CHAPTER 4: "FROM SEA TO SHINING SEA": AMERICA'S LAND AND LANDMARKS

27. Bill Fortney and David Middleton, *The Nature of North America*. New York: Watson/Guptill, 1997, p. 12.

28. Fortney and Middleton, *The Nature of North America*, p. 109.

29. Fortney and Middleton, *The Nature of North America*, p. 137.

30. Fortney and Middleton, *The Nature of North America*, p. 46.

31. Joel Garreau, *The Nine Nations of North America*. Boston: Houghton Mifflin, 1981, p. 251.

32. Quoted in Garreau, *The Nine Nations of North America*, p. 252.

CHAPTER 5: AMERICA NOW: GOVERNMENT OF, BY, AND FOR A DIVERSE PEOPLE

33. Quoted in David McCullough, *Truman*. New York: Touchstone Books/Simon & Schuster, 1992, pp. 584–85.

34. Clinton, *Between Hope and History*, p. 174.

CHAPTER 6: "I HEAR AMERICA SINGING": MANY VOICES, MANY CULTURES

35. H. L. Mencken, "Notes on Journalism," *Chicago Tribune*, September 19, 1926.

36. Walt Whitman, *Leaves of Grass*. Self-published, 1867, p. 12. www.jefferson.virginia.edu/whitman/works/leaves/1867/text/frameset.html.

37. Quoted in Richard Trenner, ed., *E. L. Doctorow, Essays and Conversations*. Princeton, NJ: Ontario Review, 1983, p. 58.

38. Quoted in Trenner, *E. L. Doctorow, Essays and Conversations*, pp. 60 and 58.

39. Quoted in Timothy Burn, "U.S. Employees Work Longer, Achieve More," *Washington Times*, September 7, 1999, p. A1.

40. Quoted in Robert Siegel, ed., *The NPR Interviews: 1995*. New York: Houghton Mifflin, 1995, p. 58.

CHRONOLOGY

1492
Columbus sails to the Bahamas.

1607
First permanent English colony is founded in Jamestown, Virginia.

1619
First colonial legislature, Virginia's House of Burgesses, meets; first black slaves are sold to Jamestown colonists.

1620
Pilgrims sail on the *Mayflower* to Cape Cod and establish colony in Plymouth, Massachusetts.

1776
American colonies declare independence from England.

1781
America wins independence from England.

1787
Constitutional Convention drafts U.S. Constitution.

1788
U.S. Constitution takes effect after ten of the original thirteen states ratify it.

1789
George Washington is elected first U.S. president.

1791
Bill of Rights becomes part of U.S. Constitution.

1803
President Thomas Jefferson authorizes the Louisiana Purchase, doubling the size of the new nation.

1846

Mexico and the United States go to war over the annexation of Texas; the United States wins two years later and Mexico cedes territory that later becomes Texas, California, Arizona, Utah, and parts of New Mexico, Colorado, and Wyoming.

1860

Lincoln is elected president; South Carolina secedes from the Union.

1861

U.S. Civil War begins as ten more states secede and form the Confederate States of America.

1863

Lincoln signs the Emancipation Proclamation, declaring slavery illegal in the Confederacy.

1865

Confederacy surrenders; Lincoln is assassinated; Thirteenth Amendment to the Constitution is adopted, abolishing slavery.

1878

Thomas Edison patents the first sound-recording device.

1879

Edison invents the first practical electric light; George Selden develops a three-cylinder combustion engine and builds first horseless carriage.

1889

The first skyscraper with an all-steel skeleton is built in Chicago.

1903

Orville and Wilbur Wright complete the world's first successful manned, powered airplane flight.

1912

Arizona becomes the forty-eighth state, the last mainland state added to the Union.

1917

United States enters World War I on the side of the Allies.

1927

Charles Lindbergh completes the first nonstop flight from New York to Paris.

1928
Walt Disney releases the first Mickey Mouse cartoon; Warner Brothers releases the first sound film, *Lights of New York.*

1929
U.S. stock market crash signals beginning of the Great Depression.

1933
President Franklin Roosevelt launches the New Deal, an array of government programs and agencies to mitigate the depression and extend government support to citizens.

1941
Japan's surprise attack on the U.S. base at Pearl Harbor, Hawaii, leads to America's entry into World War II.

1944
United States leads Allied invasion of Nazi-occupied France.

1945
Germany surrenders to the Allies; United States drops two atomic bombs on Japan, which also surrenders, ending World War II.

1947
President Harry Truman announces policy of containment against Soviet expansionism; Chuck Yeager makes first supersonic flight; Jackie Robinson becomes major league baseball's first African American player.

1950
United States enters Korean War.

1952
Korean War ends in armistice; Ernest Hemingway publishes *The Old Man and the Sea,* which helps him win the Nobel Prize for literature.

1954
U.S. Supreme Court rules that segregated schools are unconstitutional.

1955
Martin Luther King Jr. leads bus boycott in Montgomery, Alabama, launching modern civil rights movement.

1957
Congress enacts first civil rights act since the Civil War, prohibiting discrimination in public places.

1959
Alaska and Hawaii become the forty-ninth and fiftieth U.S. states.

1962
John Glenn becomes the first American to orbit Earth.

1963
President John F. Kennedy is assassinated.

1964
Congress passes new Civil Rights Act.

1968
Martin Luther King Jr. is assassinated.

1969
Apollo 11 lands first men on the Moon.

1976
United States celebrates two-hundredth anniversary.

1981
President Ronald Reagan appoints Sandra Day O'Connor to the U.S. Supreme Court, making her the first female justice.

1999
United States leads NATO to bomb the former Yugoslavia and then station peacekeeping troops to protect ethnic minorities.

SUGGESTIONS FOR FURTHER READING

Daniel J. Boorstin, *The Landmark History of the American People.* 2 vols. New York: Random House, 1968. The former U.S. Librarian of Congress offers what he calls a family album of the United States, stressing what it means to be an American; illustrated with hundreds of photographs and prints.

Sue R. Brandt, *Facts About the Fifty States.* New York: Franklin Watts, 1979. Illustrated with black-and-white photographs and charts, chronicles fun facts such as how the states were named, as well as basic information about their geography and economy.

Harold Faber, *From Sea to Sea: The Growth of the United States.* New York: Ariel Books/Farrar, Straus, and Giroux, 1995. Historian and *New York Times* reporter Harold Faber penned this geographical history, telling the story of America's regional development from the Lousiana Purchase through the acquisition of Alaska and the Pacific islands.

Charles Wright Ferguson, *Getting to Know the U.S.A.* New York: Coward-McCann, 1963. This brief book by a *Reader's Digest* editor offers a U.S. history with an emphasis on ordinary people; the author calls it a story of ordinary souls who became extraordinary as they dared to undertake tasks that the size of America demands. Includes dozens of handsome woodcut illustrations by L. E. Fisher.

Keith Lye, *United States.* New York: Franklin Watts, 1988. This oversized book offers a simple, easily accessible portrait of America with plenty of fact files and brief sidebars. It is lavishly illustrated with color and black-and-white photographs plus graphs.

WORKS CONSULTED

BOOKS

Paul M. Angle, ed., *By These Words—Great Documents of American Liberty.* New York: Rand McNally, 1968. This compendium of key U.S. documents includes the full texts of the Constitution, the Declaration of Independence, and others.

Ford R. Bryan, *Beyond the Model T: The Other Ventures of Henry Ford.* Detroit: Wayne State University Press, 1990. Focuses on Ford's experimental nature as the auto magnate led various educational and research efforts as well as nonautomotive businesses.

Bill Clinton, *Between Hope and History: Meeting America's Challenges for the Twenty-First Century.* New York: Times Books/Random House, 1996. An adaptation of major speeches by President Bill Clinton dealing with American goals and policies, both foreign and domestic.

Henry Steele Commager and Richard B. Morris, eds., *The Spirit of 'Seventy-Six: The Story of the American Revolution As Told by Participants.* New York: Harper & Row, 1976. Edited by two of America's most distinguished historians, this book contains illuminating commentaries and introductions to historical episodes based on letters, speeches, and newspapers of the Revolutionary era.

Leslie Fiedler, *An End to Innocence.* New York: Stein & Day, 1972. This literary critic's most notorious essay, "Come Back to the Raft Ag'in, Huck Honey," asserted that U.S. fiction contains a recurring theme of whites embracing minorities and together escaping from (or rebelling against) America's established society and norms.

Bill Fortney and David Middleton, *The Nature of North America.* New York: Watson/Guptill, 1997. A combined geographical survey and photo essay focusing on untouched parts of America's wilderness, created by a large team of nature writers and professional photographers. Includes a foreword by CBS News correspondent Charles Kuralt.

Russell Freedman, *Franklin Delano Roosevelt*. New York: Clarion Books/Houghton Mifflin, 1990. This simple and straightforward biography captures the robust, complex spirit of the president who led America through the Great Depression and much of World War II.

Joel Garreau, *The Nine Nations of North America*. Boston: Houghton Mifflin, 1981. A *Washington Post* reporter uses the "nine nations" metaphor to explain the unique regional cultures and characteristics of America's major sectors.

Maureen Harrison and Steve Gilbert, eds., *George Washington in His Own Words*. New York: Barnes & Noble Books, 1997. America's first president recorded his thoughts in diaries, memoranda, and speeches, including his first inaugural address, which coined the description of America as an experiment in liberty.

Richard Hofstadter, *The American Political Tradition*. New York: Random House, 1973. This political scientist's forceful essays include a particularly insightful treatment of Lincoln and the Emancipation Proclamation; rather than an expression of pure idealism, Hofstadter shows how Lincoln also freed the slaves as an expedient response to certain political and military pressures.

Bruce E. Johanson, *Forgotten Founders: Benjamin Franklin, the Iroquois, and the Rationale for the American Revolution*. Ipswich, MA: Gambit, 1982. Considering suggestions by Henry Steele Commager and others, Johanson followed the historical trail of clues to discover a surprising—and underreported—Native American influence on colonial America's evolving concept of the most desirable structure for a federal system of self-government.

Brian MacArthur, ed., *The Penguin Book of Twentieth-Century Speeches*. New York: Penguin Books, 1992. This compendium of important political and cultural speeches includes the full text of important addresses by prominent Americans and other world figures.

David McCullough, *Truman.* New York: TouchStone Books/ Simon & Schuster, 1992. This Pulitzer Prize–winning biography of American president Harry Truman sheds light on the entire U.S. political and cultural scene during the twentieth century as well as opening a global window on key events in World War II and cold war history.

John Miller, *This New Man, the American.* New York: McGraw-Hill, 1983. Miller's cultural history traces the evolution of Americanism, noting that Ben Franklin began calling himself an American as early as 1739.

Richard L. Park, ed., *The American Revolution Abroad.* Philadelphia: American Academy of Political and Social Science, 1976. A collection of scholarly essays examining how European leaders and thinkers responded to the Declaration of Independence and the Revolutionary War.

Carl Sandburg, *Abraham Lincoln—the Prairie Years and the War Years.* New York: Harcourt Brace Jovanovich, 1942. This volume of Sandburg's definitive Lincoln biography includes lengthy quotations from the Lincoln-Douglas debates and Lincoln's House, Senate, and election campaign speeches.

Robert Siegel, ed., *The NPR Interviews: 1995.* New York: Houghton Mifflin, 1995. A compendium of outstanding interviews with leading artists, politicians, scientists, and social activists.

Studs Terkel, *Chicago.* New York: Pantheon Books, 1986. A journalist and popular historian provides a literary and historical portrait of the American city that is his hometown.

Alexis de Tocqueville, *Democracy in America.* New York: HarperCollins, 1968. This French writer visited the United States in the 1830s to appraise the American character and society; many insights from this timeless classic still apply today.

Richard Trenner, ed., *E. L. Doctorow, Essays and Conversations.* Princeton, NJ: Ontario Review, 1983. A collection of interviews with the author and critical essays examining themes of his fiction.

Barbara W. Tuchman, *The First Salute.* New York: Knopf, 1988. Tuchman surveys a wide range of foreign reactions—in thought, word, and deed—to the American Revolution and the Declaration of Independence.

Frederick Jackson Turner, *The Frontier in American History.* Tucson: University of Arizona Press, 1986. Turner's well-known thesis, originally published in the 1930s, asserts that, over hundreds of years, the American frontier experience exerted broad influence on the shape and character of evolving American society in more-settled regions of the country.

Laurence Urdang, ed., *The Timetables of American History.* New York: TouchStone Books/Simon & Schuster, 1996. A fascinating and helpful reference guide, this addition to the popular Timetables series details American history year by year, chronologically correlating key events under side-by-side columns such as politics/government, literature, and everyday life.

PERIODICALS

American Historical Review, vol. 11, 1906.

Timothy Burn, "U.S. Employees Work Longer, Achieve More," *Washington Times,* September 7, 1999.

Janet Cawley, "Sandra Day O'Connor, Supreme Court Justice," *Biography Magazine,* April 1999.

Thomas L. Friedman, "An American in Paris," *New York Times,* August 20, 1999.

Lynne Heffley, "Students Find Artistic Voice in 'I, Too,'" *Los Angeles Times,* February 5, 1999, Calendar.

Joel Kotkin, "The New Ethnic Entrepreneurs," *Los Angeles Times,* September 12, 1999.

Don Lee and Nancy Cleeland, "State's Boom Brings More Job Insecurity, Study Says," *Los Angeles Times,* May 25, 1999.

H. L. Mencken, "Notes on Journalism," *Chicago Tribune,* September 19, 1926.

INTERNET AND OTHER SOURCES

Gerald R. Ford, "Remarks on Assuming the Presidency of the United States," August 9, 1974. Gerald R. Ford Library and

Museum. www.ford.utexas/edu/library/speeches/740001.
htm.

Robert L. McCan and William H. Peterson, "An Outline of the
American Economy," U.S. Information Agency, 1991.
www.usia.gov/usa/infousa/trade/ameconom/.

Robert B. Parker, "The Violent Hero: Wilderness Heritage and
Urban Reality." Ph.D. thesis, Boston University. n.d.

Lorenzo Dalla Vedova, interview with the author, Los Angeles, California, July 17, 1999.

Walt Whitman, *Leaves of Grass,* self-published, 1867. www.
jefferson.virginia.edu/whitman/works/leaves/1867/text/
frameset.html.

INDEX

PICTURE CREDITS

ABOUT THE AUTHOR

Marcus Webb is editor of *RePlay Magazine*, leading trade journal for the electronic amusements industry, and co-inventor of *Inside DVD*, the world's first digital interactive magazine on a DVD disc. His previous title for Lucent Books was *Telephones: Words Over Wires*. Mr. Webb lives in southern California.